Official Contact Pages Self-Publishing & Marketing

by James Hickman

Copyright © 2007 by James Hickman
FISRT EDITION 2007

ISBN 978-1-4243-1246-7
Library of Congress Control Number 2006907106

Published by
Bullet Entertainment Group.
5441 Riverdale Road Suite 129
College Park, GA 30349
Office: 404-246-6496
www.bentpublishing.com

All rights reserved. No part of this book may be reproduced or transmitted in any form or by any means, electronic or mechanical, including photocopying, recording, or by any information storage or retrieval system, without permission in writing from the publisher.

Though the author/publisher has made every effort to ensure the accuracy of the information within this book and data provided by its sources, some of the information may be subject to change. In the event an inaccuracy or change is located, we encourage you to contact us via web at www.bentpublishing.com so we may update our records.

Front Cover Design: James Hickman

Back Cover: James Hickman
Printed in the United States

To order additional wholesale, please contact James Hickman at 404-246-6496 or bulletent4000@yahoo.com

Acknowledgments

First of all, I give thanks to God for having a son like Jesus and watching over me all the way, and being there for me, when I was down end out. Thank you Lord. I also give thanks to my mom, mary stewart, my children Decarol, Jamarco, Frankie, James and my brothers, Anthony, Ira, Tracy, Grady.

TABLE OF CONTENTS

INTRODUCTION

1. Getting Started
    Learning the Industry 8-10
    Business Matters 10-12
    Trade Registration 12-14
    Preparing the Manuscript 15-16
    The Cover Design 17

2. Printing
    Book Manufacturers 18-19
    Preparing a Printing Estimate 19-21
    List of Book Manufacturers 22-23
    Digital Demand Publishing 23-24

3. Announcing Your Book
    Letting the Industry Know 25-26
    Pre-Publication Reviews 26-28
    Post-Publication Reviews 28-29

4. Distribution
    Conventional Channels of Distribution 30-35
    Alternative Channel of Distribution 35-37

5. Creating a Demand
    Developing a Promotional Plan 38-39
    Promotional Kit 39-41
    Way to Create a Demand 41-48
    The Internet Shipping Books 48-52

APPENDIX

5 Major Book Publishers (and their divisions) 53-59

Book Printers 60-72

Information Resources 73

ISBN and Barcode Suppliers 74-75

Book Manufacturers 76-80

Book Distributors 81-85

Publishers 86-95

Literary Agents 96-105

Suggested Resources 106-108
   Industry Resources 109-123
   E-Publishing 123-125

Glossary 126-149

Introduction

How and why I wrote this book

Among the reasons I wrote the original "official contact pages, self-publishing & marketing" was to provide and accurate resource tool to assist people in the publishing industry seeking vital information, book manufacturers, distribution, book printers, Literary agents, publishers, ISBN and barcode suppliers,
and book marketing and much more !!!
When I first came into the business, I didn't know a thing about the inner workings of the book publishing industry, so I asked a lot of people and they couldn't really provide me with complete information. Then I thought, where would I find it. So I did my own extensive research and created the official contact pages self-publishing & marketing. I developed an even stronger determination to produce the book based on my own experiences. Thank you, enjoy!

—James Hickman
Author

1. GETTING STARTED

Learning about the Industry

There are several sources of information to help you learn about the industry. Before embarking on any major project, it only makes sense to familiarize your self with the lay of the land. Contact the following organizations and publications to request membership information and magazine samples. Also request a sample of the *American Bookseller* magazine.

American Booksellers Association (ABA)
828 S. Broadway
Tarrytown, NY 10591
(800) 637-0037
www.bookweb.org.

The Web Site provides information on regional as well as independent booksellers associations.

These two associations provide co-op membership services to independent publishers.

PMA: The Independent Booksellers Association
627 Aviation Way
Manhattan Beach, CA 90266
(310) 372-2732
www.pma-online.org.

A U.S. trade association for independent publishers of video, audio, and books.

SPAN
Box 1306

Offical Contact Pages: Getting Started

Buena Vista, CO 81211
(719) 395-4790
www.spannet.org.

A non-profit trade organization that is dedicated to providing resources for authors and independent publishers.

Request sample copies of the industry's trade journals.

Publishers Weekly
Box 16178
North Hollywood, CA 91615
(800) 278-2991
www.publishersweekly.com

Independent Publisher
121 E. Front St. 4th Fl
Traverse City, MI 49684
(616) 933-0445
www.bookpublishing.com

Visit Local Bookstores. Browse the subject category of your book in bookstores. See how your idea compares with similar books on the market. Tell bookstore owners or the store managers you are publishing a book and would like their advice. You may want to call in advance to set up a convenient time to meet. After the meeting, send a thank-you note. When your book is released they may be more inclined to carry your title, especially if you used their suggestions.

Public Libraries have a wealth of free information. Visit the reference desk and become familiar with the following publications and any others they recommend for the self-publisher. Many libraries have free access to the Internet.

> **Literary Market Place: A valuable resource listing agents, associations, books clubs, reviewers, news services, radio and TV stations.**

➢ **Books in Print & Forthcoming Books:** Lists over 1 million titles currently in print in the United States. Also includes the authors' and publishers' names.

On-Line Services & the Internet. Connect electronically to people with similar interests. Various discussion groups (newsgroups) and research archives are accessible to anyone with a computer, modem and online service provider. By doing a search on words such as *self-publishing*, a subscriber can browse, research, meet, or post a question to others who may be of help. Check your phone book for local Internet Service Provider or contact any of the four national commercial providers listed below.

America Online	(800) 827-6364
CompuServe	(800) 848-8199
Microsoft Network	(800) 373-3676
Prodigy	(800) 776-3449
NetZero	(888) 349-0029
PeoplePC Online	(866) 558-7987
Earthlink	(800) 327-8454
Comcast	(800) com-cast
Verizon	(866) 232-4282
Bell South	(800) 436-8638
Alltel	(800) 245-7630

Business Matters

All too often we forget that writing is an art and publishing is a business. For practical, tax and legal reasons it is important to establish a business structure in which your publishing venture can thrive.

Think of a few names and logos with which to identify your publishing business. Avoid appearing too small by using your own name. Invent a name that is simple, easy to remember, descriptive and will not limit future publications.

Offical Contact Pages: Getting Started

Once you have narrowed your choices, check the following resources in the library to avoid name duplication with another publisher.

- **Small Press Record of Books in Print**
- **Publishers Directory by Gale Research**
- **Books in Print (Publisher listing)**

Plan a budget for publishing your book. Decisions between what you *want* and what you can *afford* will be easier with a budget. Expect to spend anywhere from $1000 to $50,000 depending on the type of book, quantity printed and marketing plans. Three major areas of expense will be:

Book Preparation   -   Printing   -   Promotion

NOTE: A general guideline for planning the promotional budget is to set aside $1.00 per book printed.

Apply for a business license with your state and local governments. Before you apply, decide on a type of business structure: Sole Proprietorship, Partnership, or Corporation. Most first time publishers choose Sole Proprietorship because it is the easiest. Talk to a banker, lawyer, or the Small Business Administration for advice on starting a business.

Small Business Administration (SBA)
200 N. College St. #A2015
Charlotte, NC 28202
(800) 827-5722 (Answer Desk)
www.sba.gov

Protect your privacy and **rent a box from the Post Office** for your mailing address. Request information on bulk mailing permits as well as postal rates. Postage will be a major expense, so know your options to manage mailing costs.

Professionalize your business image with stationary. Print letterheads, envelopes, business cards and shipping labels with your name, address and logo. Project an image which will instill confidence in people who may want to do business with you. Single title author-publishers must overcome the stigma of being perceived as unprofessional.

TRADE REGISTRATIONS

The **International Standard Book Number (ISBN)** is the ten digit number on the back of every book. **(January 1, 2007 the ISBN will become a 13 digit number)** The numbers identify the publisher and the book title. The book trade uses this number to order, price and keep track of inventory. Most wholesalers and bookstores are reluctant to stock a book that does not have this number clearly printed on the back cover. The numbers are available through R.R. Bowker. There is a handling fee of about $300 and you will receive 10 sets of ISBN numbers. They will arrive on a computer printout sheet reserved for your selection. The remaining nine set of numbers can be used for revised editions and future publications.

After you select a number from the computer printout sheet, activate by completing the **Advance Book Information (ABI)** form included with you ISBN order. By submitting an ABI form, your book will be listed in *Books in Print* at no charge. Call R.R. Bowker and request a publisher's information packet on how to apply an ISBN number.

R.R. Bowker (ISBN Agency)
121 Chanlon Rd.
New Providence, NJ 07974
877-310-7333
www.bowker.com/standards/home/isbnusisbnqa.html

Offical Contact Pages: Getting Started

Set a publication date far enough in the future to give you time to print, submit for review, announce your book and generate advance sales. Your publication date is not the date your book comes back from the printer. The publication date is when you are releasing your book for sale to the public. The best publication date for the self-publisher is the first quarter of the year and still be new. The two major buying seasons for the publishing industry are Spring and Fall.

Copyright protection lasts your life plus 50 years. This is done by using the copyright symbol with the year and your name and including it on the copyright page of your manuscript. Also, when your manuscript is complete, send yourself a *notarized* copy by *registered mail* and place unopened in storage. This is evidence of a specific date within the copyright office in Washington, DC. Order in advance the circulars on Copyright and form TX which is package #109. They are free of charge. Call (202) 707-9100 or visit their website:

- **Registrar of Copyrights**- Library of Congress
  www.lcweb.loc.gov/copyright

- **Trademark Patent** (800) 786-9199
  If you plan to make sales to the library market, apply for a **Library of Congress Card Catalog Number (LCCN)** and a publisher's **Catalog in Publication (CIP)**. These numbers will go on the copyright page of your book. There is no charge for the LCCN and a nominal charge for the CIP number. Request information from the following:

  Pre-assigned LCCN Number:

  Library of Congress
  Cataloging in Publication Division
  Washington DC 20540
  (202) 707-2223/ (202) 707-5959

CIP number for single title publisher:

Quality Books
1003 W. Pines RD
Oregon, IL 61061
(815) 732-4450

Barcodes (Bookland EAN) are those vertical lines on the back of books. This enables a price scanner to identify the title, ISBN number and price. The cost is about $40. You will need the ISBN number before you can order one. Bookland EAN has become a requirement by most of the book trade.

Data Index, Inc.
Box 1647
Snohomish WA 98292
(800) 426-2183
www.dataindex.com

Fotel-GGX Associates, Inc
41 W. Home Ave
Villa Park, IL 60181
(800) 834-4920
www.fotel.com

PREPARING THE MANUSCRIPT

If you use other people's words (not ideas) in your book, you must get permission. Send a request to the publisher by certified mail stating what you want to quote, how you will use it and where you will give credit. Normally you will get permission without cost. Copying and selling words of another author without permission is called plagiarism and is illegal.

Editing. A Copy editor can clarify and strengthen what you want to say and how you say it. This includes clarity, consistency and the overall correctness of the manuscript. Contact a local newspaper or magazine to see if an editor or writer is willing to find an English teacher or graduate student from a local college who would love to receive acknowledgment in your book in exchange for assistance. Also, see the Yellow Pages for "Editorial Services" listing.

In editing: review slowly, question everything and ask yourself, "Are the statements I am making true and verifiable?"

Have a competent person proofread your manuscript for grammar, spelling, usage and punctuation. Do not rely on your computer's spell checker since it does not know whether you want to use "to", "too", or "two". It is quite common to rewrite your manuscript several times before it is ready to print . . .so be patient. Changes become costly after the manuscript goes to the printer. Include those people who help in the book's acknowledgments.

NOTE: *Realize how editing and proofreading influence the quality of your book. Seek competent help in these areas to reduce post-printing regrets.*

Typesetting & Layout. This has to do with the selection and placement of your illustrations, graphs, pictures and text. In other words: how the inside of your book will look. The goal of the layout design is to communicate a consistent visual message throughout the book, making it easier to read and use. Browse books in bookstores and libraries to use as models for you own layout. A professional typesetter's fee can range from $4-10 per page. Thus, it may be cost-effective to purchase a computer, desktop software and even a printer to do it yourself. Today's laser printers can produce clear camera-ready 600 DPI (dots per inch) text output at a reasonable price.

Contact www.BentPublishing.com

Page Layout Margins. The layout margin is the space between the edge of the paper and where the text starts. That compensates for trimming during the printing process. Typically a .5 to 1.5 inch margin is adequate, depending on the design, size of book an type of binding you use. For example, this book uses a .625 inch margin.

Typeface & Font. Most books use a Serif typeface for the main body of the text instead of sans serif type because it is easier to read and looks more professional. See the samples below. Handwritten copy or calligraphy may be suitable for certain publications, such as children's books or poetry. However, too much handwritten copy is hard to read and may detract from the flavor and intention of your book.

Serif   sans serif

Illustrations. Illustrations can range from charts, photographs and artwork to anything that is not typeset. In planning the layout, leave enough space for the illustrations and either scan them in with a computer or paste them in by hand. Contact book manufactures for preferred format.

THE COVER DESIGN

The goal of the cover design is to get people's attention. Books are often sold on the merits of the cover alone; thus, the cover should capture the essence of your book. It is well worth the investment to hire a graphic artist with book design experience. Expect to pay $500 for a basic one color design to over $2500 for an eye-catching full color camera-ready design.

Contact: www.BentPublishing.com

People's first impressions come from the title of your book. Keep your book title brief, vivid and descriptive. The title should be legible from 10 Feet so people strolling though the bookstore can read it at a glance. The subtitle gives you an added sales message, describing your book in greater detail. Once you have narrowed possible book titles, check *Books in Print* and *Forthcoming Books* to avoid title duplication.

If you think the book's **spine** is unimportant in the design, consider how many books in a bookstore are faced out that way. Include on the spine the title of the book, author's and publisher's names and logo.

The **back cover** should convince the potential book buyers they are making the right decision by purchasing your book. Make it easy, interesting and informative for the browser to review. The back cover might include:

- Book's description and benefits to the reader
- Reviews, Endorsements and Testimonials
- Author's bio and picture
- ISBN, Bar Code, Price and Subject Category

The easiest way to get **testimonials or endorsements** is to ask for them. Ask experts or celebrities in your field to review your manuscript and submit their impressions. Get permission in writing to print their comments on your book cover.

2. PRINTING

Book Manufacturers

Get bids from Book Manufacturer instead of a local printer. Book manufacturers have the equipment to print and bind books themselves, instead of sending out the work and marking up the price. If your book is more than 50 pages and you are printing more than 200 copies, chanced are the prices will be much lower through a book manufacturer.

Cheapest isn't always best. Consider quality, service and support. If a problem arises – and printing is fertile ground for problems- whose side will your printer be on, yours or his? Paying a little more for peace of mind is often worth it. Request samples and check references before you decide.

Request *blueline* proofs and *cover matchprint* from your printer before your book goes to final press. This means you'll see and approve what the text and cover will look like before it is printed. This is also the time to check for typographical errors or pages missing or out sequence. There may be a charge for this service, but it is comforting to have the chance to make last minute changes.

Most printers will print about 10% too many or too few books. These are called over- or under-runs. Ask what the over-runs will cost. They usually cost less, thus lowering the overall cost from the same printer because of reduced setup costs. Still, get other quotes to keep everyone honest.

It's more economical to print in even signatures. This means the number of pages a printing press can print at one time. Most book manufacturers use a 16 or 32 page signature, depending on the size of the book (for example: 32 for 8.5x 5.5 and 16 for 8.5 x 11). Divide the pages of your book by 16 or 32 and you will know how many signatures

Offical Contact Pages: Printing

the printer will use. If your book is a page or two over an even signature, reduce the printing cost by editing them out.

Retail Price. Search bookstores for comparable books to use as price models. A common mistake for self-publishers is to price their book either too high or too low. Printing costs do affect the retail price of the book. Don't expect your first printing to be very profitable, particularly when printing a small quantity. Reprints are far more profitable because of reduced printing costs, assuming you don't make too many changes to the book. Set a cover price that would allow for a profit, giving a 55% discount for distribution.

Preparing a Printing Estimate

To prepare a price quote from a book manufacturer, you will need to know:

- Quantity
- Total page count
- Type of paper (text and cover)
- How many colors on the cover and cover coating
- Type of binding
- Size of the book
- Number of pictures (black and white or color)
- Packaging and shipping costs

Quantity. How many books should you order? The more you print, the less each costs. Strike a balance between printing enough copies to keep your unit cost down and too many copies where you are stuck with a garage full of unsold books. Typically, small publishers will order between 500 and 3500 books in the first printing. The only time to order more is if most are pre-sold. You can always re-order when your inventory gets low. Remember, reprints generally cost less barring many changes. Changes require the cost of new printing plates. Plan on a 3 to 5 week wait for delivery.

Page Count. To figure the total page count in your book, include the *front* and the *back matter*. The *front matter* is all the pages before the main text: Title Pages, Copyright Page, Acknowledgments, Preface, Foreword, Introduction, Table of Contents and Dedication. The *back matter* includes all pages in a book after the main text: Afterword, Appendix, Bibliography, Glossary and Index.

Paper. Unless you are doing an art of full color specialty book, most printers will suggest a 50, 60, or 70lb. white offset. 60 lb. paper is most common. The higher the weight, the heavier and more opaque the paper will be. The thickness (bulk) of the paper is measured by PPI (pages per inch). The lower the PPI, the bulkier the paper, thus, the thicker the book. Ask the printer for this number to determine the width of the book's spine.

NOTE: One of your greatest expenses will be postage and shipping. The paper you select will influence this expense. Heavier paper costs more to ship.

Cover Paper. Will the book be softcover of hardcover? Because of lower production costs, most books are now softcover. The standard paper for softcover is a 10 or 12 point C1S (coated one side) cover stock. Hardcover books will use a dust jacket, and 80 or 100 lb enamel paper is most common. Order five to ten percent extra book covers or dust jackets, as they are useful for various promotional purposes.

Cover Coating. This is what protects the book cover and enhances the color. There are various kinds available: Lay flat plastic film lamination, matted, aqueous coating or

Offical Contact Pages: Printing

UV. Ask the printers what type they use and the advantages of each. Request samples. This book uses film lamination.

Binding. This is what holds the book together. Some common types are Perfect Bound (softcover), Otabind (softcover that lies open), Case Bound (hardcover), Spiral or Saddle Stitched (stapled). How the book will be used will influence the type of binding. This book is Perfect Bound.

NOTE: Bookstores frown upon Spiral and Saddle Stitched books because you can't read them when faced spine out on the shelf.

Book Size. The conventional and common 5.5 x 8.5 is suitable for both hard and softcover, and is one of the most economical to print. Other standard sizes include 6 x 9 and 8.5 x 11. The further you get away from the standard, the more expensive the book is to produce.

Pictures. Color photos can be beautiful, although the cost may be prohibitive because of color separation and extra print run fees. B&W photos are mare practical and affordable. All B&W photos require halftones. The process of creating a halftone converts the picture into dots of various sizes and shades of gray. Most halftones for books are produced at 120-133 dots per inch. Consult your graphic artist and book manufacturer for a recommendation.

Packaging. Ask your printer the most economical way to ship your books. Plan for storage by asking the printer the size and weight of the cartons. A packaging option to consider is shrink wrapping. This is a clear plastic wrap used to protect the books and should be considered if you intend to store your books in a garage or unheated area.

List of Book Manufactures

These printers specialize in the manufacturing of books. For additional listings, see the *Literary Market Place* in a library. Get all estimates **in writing** before you make a decision. Printing estimates are available online.

Bang Printing
1473 Highway 18
Brainerd, MN 56401
(218) 829-2877
www.bangprinting.com

Edwards Brothers
2500 S State ST Ann Arbor, MI 48106
(313) 769-1000
www.edwardbrothers.com

Gilliland Printing
215 N. Summit Arkansas City, KS 67005
(800) 323-8200
www.gilprin.com

Malloy Lithographing
5411 Jackson RD
Ann Arbor, MI 48103
(800) 722-3231
www.malloy.com

McNaughton & Gunn
960 Woodland Dr.
Saline, MI 48176
(734) 429-5411
www.bookprinters.com

Sheridan Books
613 E Industrial Dr.
Chelsea, MI 48118
(734) 475-9145
www.sheridanbook.com

Thomson-Shore
7300 W Joy RD
Dexter, MI 48130
(734) 426-3939
www.tshore.com

United Graphics
2916 Marshall Ave
Mattoon, IL 61938
(217) 235-7161
www.unitedgraphicsinc.com

Ultra Short-Run Book Printers (200 to 1000 copies)

C & M Press
4825 Nome St Denver, CO 80239
(303) 375-9922
www.cmpress.com

BentPublisher
5441 Riverdale Rd.
College Park, GA
404-246-6496
www.bentpublishing.com

Offical Contact Pages: Printing

Gorham Printing
334 Harris RDRochester, WA 98579
(800) 837-0970

South OF Harlem
5285 Lake Rock Way
Atlanta, Ga. 30311
(404) 642-9629
www.southofharlem.com

Digital Demand Printing

Digital technology is quickly changing the way books are produced, published, and distributed. On-line publishing has become an attractive alternative to the high costs of conventional publishing, making it easier for writers to become published authors. The two general ways are:

Electronic Books. This is when you submit your manuscript in a digital word processing format, then your manuscript is converted into a document people can purchase over the Internet. Electronic books are sometimes call eBooks, virtual books, digital books or on-line books. eBooks are paperless. They are a full-length manuscript which is downloaded as a data file directly to the purchaser's computer. The self publisher retains all rights and is free to print through conventional means if the demand warrants. The cost to produce an eBook is considerably less than conventional means. Fees typically run under $1000.

eBook publishing is a prudent way to test market your book or publish when there is a specialized or limited audience. Since there is no inventory, an eBook is sold for significantly less than a traditional hard or softcover copy. Orders are handled through a contracted eBook distributor, then a royalty is paid to you for each sale. Royalties range from 30% to 50%. Even though your eBook will be made available through many on-line bookstores, it is still in the self-publisher's interest to actively promote the eBook.

Print-on-Demand (POD). Most eBook distributors can also print your book in a hard or softcover version. Print-on-Demand means your book is printed and shipped t the quantity ordered. If a bookstore wants to purchase a single copy of your book, it is able to order without the transaction going through you. This eliminated the self-publisher's cost of inventory, shipping and returns. If the demand for your book becomes substantial, then printing through conventional means may be justified.

Certain constraints do exist with POD technology. Books must be more than one hundred pages and with few photographs. Although the photo reproduction technology is improving, pictures lack the crispness of lithography. POD Books carry a higher retail price to compensate for production, convenience, wholesale discounts and a profit. Many eBooks distributors have contracted with Ingram Book Company's Lightning Print on Demand Distribution Program making your book available to any bookstore nationwide.

The following companies specialize in the production and distribution of eBooks. See *Literary Market Place* in the library for additional listings.

1st Books Library
2511 E 3rd STBloomington, IN 47403
(800) 839-8640
www.1stbooks.com

toExcel
165 W95th ST #B-NNew York, NY 10025
(877) 288-4737
www.toexcel.com

POD technology is the future of book printing. As this technology matures, bookstores will be able to produce hard or softcover editions of any book in digital format with electronic kiosks. The customer can view a portion, or the entire book, read reviews and order right on the spot. Depending on your book's purpose and marketing plans, it still may be more advantageous to print, inventory, distribute and promote through traditional means.

Offical Contact Pages: Announcing Your Book

3. Announcing Your Book

Letting the Industry Know

Let the book trade know that you have published a book. Orders can come most unexpectedly by having your title listed in several directories. Most of these listings are free. Write or phone to request an application.

International Standard Book Numbering Agency (ISBN) When you submit your ABI (Advanced Book Informational) Form with your publication date and ISBN number, you will automatically be listed in *Books in Print.*

Library of Congress Catalog Card Number. When you request an LC number, you book will be listed in a catalog enabling libraries to locate your book more easily.

Cumulative Book Index & Vertical File Index
H.W. Wilson Co.
950 University Ave.
Bronx, NY 10452
(718) 588-8400
www.hwwilson.com

Small Press Record of Books in Print & International Directory of Little Magazines and Small Presses.

Dustbooks
Box 100
Paradise, CA 95967
(530) 877-6110
www.dustbooks.com

ABA Books Buyers Handbook
American Booksellers Assn.
828 S. Broadway
Tarrytown, NY 10591
(800) 637-0037
www.bookweb.org

Gale Directories
Publishers Directory
27500 Drake Rd.
Farmington Hill, MI 48331
(800) 347-4253
www.galegroup.com

Pre-Publication Reviews

Besides yourself, who will think your book is great? Prepublication reviews are directed at the trade (libraries, wholesalers, bookstores) before the publication date and the release of your book. This helps the trade evaluate new titles, and influences its purchasing decisions.

Trade Reviews. To be reviewed, at least 90 days before the publication date, the major trade review magazines want to see: a galley (NOT a finished book), sample cover (if available), a fact sheet (describing the features of the book such as title, subtitle, description, page count, ISBN and LC numbers, binding, price and wholesale availability), author's bio, any endorsements from respected authorities and publicity plans. Write a brief cover letter stating what the book is about, why you wrote it and how it is unique from others on the market. Send all this by first mail. This is no guarantee your book will be reviewed. However, even one favorable review could generate substantial advance sales. In addition, any reviews you receive can be used on your promotional literature and printed on the back cover of reprinted books. It is worth a phone call to inquire about the full name (with correct spelling) of the person to whom you will submit a review package. Also, inquire about any special submission guidelines. Follow up all submissions with a finished book. See *Literary Market Place* for additional review source.

Booklist/American Library Assn.
50 E. Huron ST Chicago, IL 60611
(312) 944-6780
www.ala.org

Bloomsbury Review
1553 Platte ST.
#206 Denver, CO 80202
(303) 455-3123
www.bookforum.com/

Offical Contact Pages: Announcing Your Book

Chicago Tribune Books
435 N Michigan Ave.
Chicago, IL 60611
(312) 222- 3232
www.chicagotribune.com

Independent Publish
121 E. Front ST. 4th Fl
Traverse City, MI 49684
(616) 633-0445
www.bookpublishing.com

Library Journal
245 W. 17th ST
New York, NY 10011
(212) 463-6818
www.libraryjournal.com

N.Y. Times Book Review
229 W. 43rd ST
New York, NY 10036
www.nytimes.com

Publishers Weekly
245 W. 17th ST   New York, NY 10011
(212) 463-6758
www.publishersweekly.com

School Library Journal
245 W. 17th ST   New York, NY 10011
(212) 463-6759
www.slj.com

N.Y. Review of Books
1755 Broadway New York, NY 10019
(212) 757-8070
www.nybooks.com

L.A. Times Book
Times Mirror SquareLos Angeles, CA 90053

San Francisco Chronic Book Review
901 Mission ST San Francisco, CA 94
(415) 777-7042
www.sfgate.com

> finished book. Instead of paying to have galley proofs printed and bound, consider making copies of your camera-randy manuscript you furnished the printer.

A News Release. A news release is a one page (double spaced) write-up about your book. Your release should reflect the personality of your book by building around one central theme. Write in the inverted pyramid style, with the most important information at the top, followed by more specific details. Make the release sound like news and avoid "hype". Get to the point quickly. A news release is not advertising copy; it is designed to report information. Keep to the facts, leaving out flowery adjectives, superlatives and opinion. Answer throughout the release, the *Who, What, When, Where* and *Why* (or How) about the book. With so many books vying for publicity, what is it about your book that gives it news value (information which excites the reviewer)?

Post-Publication Reviews

Post-publication reviews are intended to reach the purchaser of your book. It is very expensive and inefficient to send review copies to every book reviewer. Target those from whom you have the best chance of getting a review.

Giving Review Copies Away. Giving books away can become an expensive proposition, particularly when you include the cost of postage. A simple rule is to budget at least 10% of the books from you first printing as review copies and give them to the people who can do you the most good. Despite the expense, giving away review copies can be an extremely good promotional investment. Stamp REVIEWCOPY, NOT FOR SALE on any copy you give away to discourage people from selling or returning that book to a wholesaler for a refund. Keep good records of giveaways as they are a tax-deductible business expense.

Newspapers. Most newspaper book reviews receive more solicitations each week that they can review each month. Review space is at a premium. Nevertheless, any mention of your book will help sales. If your book has a wide general appeal, mail a news release and book request post card (or book) to the major daily newspapers, targeting the appropriate editor (Food, Features, Business, etc). Rent a mailing list from one of the mailing list managers. Local newspapers magazines are your best bets to get a book review or a news article. Because you are local news, they may be inclined to give you preference over others.

Experts in the Field. Send a review copy to authorities or experts on the subject of your book, asking for

Offical Contact Pages: Announcing Your Book

their endorsements. This is a wonderful way to get influential people talking about you book. See *Contemporary Authors* at the library for their names and mailing addresses.

Magazine Reviews. Target magazines where subscribers' interests match the subject of your book. Find out what magazines they read and send a copy of your book and a press release to those magazines' book review editors. See the *Standard Periodical Directory* in the public library for listings of specialty magazines.

Newsletter Reviews. The number of newsletters has boomed during the past decade, now accounting for nearly one-third of all publications. This has resulted in more opportunities to get your book mentioned or reviewed. In addition, most associations publish a newsletter which is mailed to their members and often has a book review section. See the *Oxbridge Directory of Newsletters* and *Encyclopedia of Associations* in the library.

Free-Lance Reviews. If your book is of general interest, rent a mailing list of free-lance book reviewers around the country (see page 54 for mailing lists brokers). Send a news release, fact sheet, and a book request return postcard (or book) immediately upon the book's release.

Book Review Tips

- Choose only those reviewers most suitable to the subject of your book.

- Follow up immediately with anyone who requests a review copy of your book.

- Don't be surprised if you don't get an overwhelming response from reviewers.

4. Distribution

How are people going to find your book if they decide to buy it? Reviews, publicity, and advertising are worthless unless your book is readily available to the reader. At least 2-6 months before the release date, decide on how you will distribute your book, whether through conventional, alternative or a combination of both channels of distribution. It is in the self-publisher's interest to use a variety of distribution channels.

Consignments. This is standard inventory stocking practice in the publishing industry, especially in the conventional channels of distribution. What this means is you don't get paid until after you book has been sold and shipped from their warehouse. Not until then are you paid (usually 90-120 days later to allow time to deduct for any returns). All unsold books are returned to you when the demand ceases. A 15-25% return rate is common, so the lack of promotion will only increase the return rate.

Promotional Plan. Most channels of distribution want to know how you are going to create a demand for your book of the stock it. That's right: the self-publisher is responsible for creating the demand. Before you approach the conventional channels of distribution, have a step-by-step promotional plan for book which answers.

Who is your target audience?
Where are they to be found?
What will be done to create a demand?

Conventional Channels of Distribution

Bookstores. There are many kinds of bookstores: General, Used, College and Religious to list just a few. Independently owned bookstores make up a shrinking half

Offical Contact Pages: Distribution

their selection process. The following are common types of distributors:

Mass Market Distributors. If your book fits their forma, they will place your title in non-bookstore locations such as supermarkets, airports, and newsstands. Their fee is 55% off list. *Require* all returns in resalable condition. Mass Market distributors traditionally have a high return rate and a short shelf life. If a book doesn't sell fast, it is replaced.

Specialty Distributors. When your book is targeted toward a specific market niche or subject area (Outdoor, Health, Ethnic etc.), specialty distributors can help you reach that reader. Their discounts vary between 55% - 65% off list.

Library Distributors. They specialize in selling books to libraries. Contact the two distributors listed below and ask for a vendor application. Both work on consignment and require a 55% discount.

Quality Books
  1003 W. Pines Rd.
Oregon, IL 61061
(815) 732-4450
www.quality-books.com

Baker & Taylor, Inc.
1120 Route 22 E
Bridgewater, NJ 08807
908-218-3803
www.btol.com

Brodart Books
500 Arch Street
Williamsport, PA 17701
(800) 233-8467
www.brodart.com

Unique Books
5010 Kemper Ave.
St. Louis, MO 63139
(314) 776-6695
Attn: Book Buyer Dept.

The Booksource Inc.
1230 Macklind Ave.
St. Louis, MO 63110
(800) 444-0435
www.booksource.com

.A. Majors Company
1401 Lakeview Dr.
Lewisville, TX 75057
(800) 633-1851
www.majors.com

Ingram Book Company
1 Ingram Blvd.
Lavernge, TN 37086
615-793-5000
www.ingrambooks.com

Master Distributors. If your book is of general interest and you plan to promote your title nationally, consider a mater distributor to carry your book. A master distributor will get your book into the major regional and national book wholesalers and perhaps present your title to major independent and chain bookstores. A Master distributor will coordinate you promotional efforts with his national sales rep network. They want a 63% - 67% discount off the list price, and may add monthly fees. Below are six master distributors to request information about their title acquisition procedure. Most will want an exclusive right to sell to the book trade (bookstores and libraries). That leaves you to sell through alternative channels. Most master distributors prefer publishers with more than one title. Have a *detailed* promotional plan before approaching these distributors.

Book World Services

Independent Publishers Group

1933 Whitfield Park Loop
Sarasota, FL 34243
(941) 758-8094
www.bookworld.com

814 N Franklin ST
Chicago, IL 60610
(312) 337-0747
www.ipgbook.com

Login Publishers Consortium Network

National Book

1436 W. Randolph ST
Chicago, IL 60607
(312) 432-7650
www.lb.com

4720 Boston Way
Lanham, MD 20706
(301) 459-3366
www.nbnbooks.com

Offical Contact Pages: Distribution

Access Publishers Network West
6893 Sullivan Rd.
Grawn, MI 49637
(616) 276-5196
www.accesspublishers.com

Publishers Group
1700 4th ST
Berkeley, CA94710
(510) 528-1444
www.pgw.com

Alternative Channels of Distribution

If your book does not have a broad, general appeal for conventional channels of distribution, all is not lost. Most books sold in the United States are sold through alternative channels. Books on a specific subject or tight market niche may find alternative channels the easiest to secure and most profitable. Consult the *Literary Market Place* for additional listings of alternative channels of distribution.

Book Clubs. Book clubs may be interested in purchasing book club rights or actual copies of your book when printed. While come special interest book clubs will buy books regardless of the publication date, most prefer 6 months notice before the publication date.

Catalog Houses. Have you ever received a catalog in the mail that featured books? Thousands of companies in the United States send out catalogs annually, many including books. Send a copy of your book to mail order catalog companies that specialize in the subject area of your title. For mail order catalogs that feature books, see *The Directory of Mail Order Catalogs* and *Literary Market Place* at the public library. Visit www.buyersindex.com on the Internet for a listing of more than 5000 catalog companies by specialty.

Gift Stores. Over 30% of the population have never been in a bookstore. Having your book displayed in retail outlets such as gift and card shops is a way to reach some of those people. However, the discount is a little higher, generally 50% off list. Most gift stores prefer buying through gift reps. Many large cities have wholesale gift-center showrooms where manufacturers and gift rep organizations display their wares for wholesale purchase. Check phonebook.

Special Sales. Home improvement centers, drugstores, auto supply dealers, kitchen shops and health food stores are all prospects if your book firs their market. In other words, approach people or companies who can tie your book into the marketing of their own products. Most of these sales are made on a non-returnable basis at a negotiated discount.

Fulfillment Services. These companies offer warehousing and order-processing services (toll-free number & credit card purchases over the phone) for your book. Most want a percentage and/ or a monthly fee for their service. As you promote your title, make reference to the service's toll-free number for ordering 24 hours a day. Contact the following:

Publication Services
8803 Tara LN
Austin, TX 78737
(512) 288-5021
www.psifulfillment.com

Upper Access
85 Upper Access Rd.
Hinesburg, VT 05461
(802) 482-2988
www.upperaccess.com

The Intrepid Group
1331 Red Cedar CR
Ft. Collins, CO 80524
(970) 493-3793
www.intrepidgroup.com

BookMasters
2541 Ashland Rd.
Mansfield, OH 44905
(419) 589-5100
www.bookmasters.com

On-line Bookstores (Internet). These are businesses that have a website on the Internet and will list your book in their electronic bookstore. People around the world can browse a book's contents, read excerpts, and get ordering information from their computer. Watch for special interest bookstores that are emerging on the Web that may closely match your book's market niche. Be cautious about signing any exclusive agreement to your book's electronic rights.

Offical Contact Pages: Distribution

Also worth a visit: www.booksense.com, www.fatbrain.com, and www.allbookstores.com.

Subsidiary Rights. This is when you sell the rights of all or a portion of your book to someone else who will package it in a different form for his market. Some examples include: movie / TV rights, an excerpt for a magazine article, paperback or hardcover rights, electronic rights and foreign rights. Consider hiring an agent or attorney familiar with the right you are selling. See *Literary Market Place* in the Library.

Remainder Dealers. Remainder dealer help liquidate overstocks and remaining copies of your out-of-print books. They will purchase unsold books at pennies on the dollar. When all sales sources are exhausted, contact several remainder dealers to see who will give you the best price and terms. See *Literary Market Place* in the library.

Donations. Another way to liquidate unsold books is to donate remaining and damaged books to q worthy cause or non-profit groups and take the tax write-off.

5. Creating a Demand

Developing a Promotional Plan

Promoting a book is generally the most important and demanding function for a self-publisher. There are more than 2000 new titles released each week, nearly two million books in print, and the average bookstore stocks only 50,000 titles. This contributes to a very crowded and competitive arena. The book trade has just one question: **"Will your book sell?"**

A book is a product, and like any other product it requires publicity and promotion. Potential readers must be made aware of your book, how it differs from similar books on the market and where they can purchase it. Proper planning is essential to give your book the best chance of success.

A Promotional Plan. This answers the questions: **Who** is your target audience? **Where** are they found? **What** will be done to create a demand?

WHO is your audience and **WHERE** are they found? Typically, there are multiple audiences for your book. A technique to help you figure out Who will buy your book is to spend time in the library compiling lists of organizations, associations, corporations, hobbyists, occupations, experts and anyone else who you want to reach first, second, third, etc. Review the list and see if there is any overlap. This will help you direct your efforts more efficiently and give you insight into the best ways to reach them.

The self-publisher actually has two categories of customers: **The Trade** and **The Reader.** The Trade consists

Offical Contact Pages: Creating a Demand

of bookstores, wholesalers and libraries. The Reader is your target audience or end user. Research and promotional efforts must be allocated to both, particularly when pursuing conventional channels of distribution.

When is the Trade and the Reader in the most favorable buying mood? Does your book have a seasonal twist? Publishers introduce new release throughout the year with an emphasis on two seasons: Spring and Fall. The industry's largest trade show, Book Expo America (formally the ABA), occurs annually around the end of May. This is a key time for publishers to show their new titles to the Trade. Readers purchase books throughout the year with an emphasis on the holiday and gift seasons. The nature of your book is also a consideration as the timing may be built into your product and those you intend to reach.

WHAT will be done to create a demand? How will you let the reader know about your book and where to purchase copies? There are six general ways to reach the Reader through your promotions: *Mail, Fax, Phone, Computer, The Media* and *In Person*, each having its cost advantages and disadvantages. People today are more accessible, yet harder to sell, stressing the importance of a tightly targeted and strong sales message. The remaining chapter will outline what you will need to promote your book, and the numerous ways to create a demand. With so many options, self-publishers have the luxury of time to systematically test several promotional options to find what works best. What works for one book may not work for another, thus the importance of proper planning. In the end, tracking sales will clearly define to whom and where your book will sell. Thus, you can adjust your promotional strategy accordingly.

Promotional Kit

There is no limit to what you can spend on promotional materials. It becomes a question of budget and what is practical. The following are suggestions for a basic promotional kit for the budget minded self-publisher.

- ➢ **News Release**. The one page (double-spaced) news release answers why you wrote the book, concentrating on what issue, solution or benefit your book will address for the Reader. This is what is mailed to announce the release of your book to reviewers, bookstores and the media. Keep it simple, factual, informative, and interesting.

- ➢ **Extra Book Covers**. Extra book covers come in handy as mailers or point of purchase display and can be used part of your media kit. Many distributors will request extra covers for their sales force to use to sell your title.

- ➢ **Media Kit**. A Media Kit (often termed Press Kit) simply provides more information about you and your book. This gives an editor, producer, reporter, or interviewer useful information for a book review, interview or article. In a glossy 8 x 11pocket folder, include: A book, news release, author bio, photo, fact sheep, any reviews, news articles, endorsements and sample interview questions. The key is for the information to be well organized and easy to read as most interviewers will not read your book.

- ➢ **Fact Sheet**. A fact sheet outlines the basic features or facts of your book. On one page, include: title, subtitle, author, brief book description, ISBN /LC number, publication date, book size, page count, type of binding, weight, number of books per case and wholesale availability. The fact sheet answers important questions for reviewers, the media, editors, vendors and the book trade.

- ➢ **Photos.** Most interviewers want to know what you look like. Purchase 5 x 7 black & white promotional glossies of yourself that complement the message of your book. Pictures are often requested by reviewers, magazines, newspapers and even bookstores to promote your signing.

Offical Contact Pages: Creating a Demand

NOTE: Label all photos with a sticker on the back with book title, author's name and phone number. This will help avoid misplacement.

- **Reviews, Endorsements/ & Letters.** Save any reviews, endorsements, testimonials, fan mail and articles written about you or your book. These provide great sales copy for your promotional literature.

- **Book Request Postcard.** Print book request return postcards and include one with your news release when you are not sending a review copy of your book. Those interested in your news release message will respond, thus saving you the expense of mailing books randomly to uninterested people.

- **Brochure, Flyer, or Postcard.** A full-color flyer is useful, catchy and profession. A helpful hint is to leave some blank space on the front of the back side to photocopy a specific promotional message and use for many promotional situations. A 4 x 6 color post card with your book cover printed on one side and a sales message on the other can save on postage and envelope costs. Shop around, as prices vary from printer to printer.

Ways to Create a Demand

Promotion and publicity are essential to your books' success. However, no one can predict the commercial success of a book. You can only give your book the best possible chance to succeed with the least amount of risk; then wait for the market to send its verdict. This section will outline the many ways you can create a demand for your book.

Author's Tours. Do you like to travel? Does your book have a broad appeal? If so, author's tours can be a rewarding, although expensive, endurance test, but one of the best ways to reach a large book buying public. Pick the destination(s), and at least 6 week in advance, book yourself on as many TV and radio shows as possible. Inform all bookstores (in each area) of your promotional activity, encouraging them to have your book in stock. Select the area's most popular bookstore in which to do a lecture or reading and book signing. Send notices to local newspapers outlining your activity, as they any be interested in an interview or at least a mention in their paper. Always bring extra books so you won't run out.

Book Signings. Unless your signing is backed by a great deal of media promotion, it is doubtful that people will be lined up waiting for you autograph. However, a signing serves many purposes. Your book will be displayed in the store. You begin building a relationship with the store owner, manager and staff (who can recommend your title to their customers) and leave behind signed copies, which increases the book's appeal. Most bookstores are receptive to signings, as your presence will help pull customers into their store, resulting in free publicity for both you and them. Send the local media advance notice of your signing as most will list this free of charge.

Book Signing Party. Kick off the release of your book with a book signing party at your home, office or local bookstore, Gather friends, family, neighbor, associates, colleagues and anyone else who would support you and your book's message, Invite the local media.

Seminars. If you enjoy teaching and speaking, find a group, business, college or organization to sponsor and promote your seminar. This will help offset any costs incurred and provide a built-in endorsement for you and your book.

Readings & Lectures. Local social, civic, and business organizations are all looking for speakers. Use your expertise to promote your book. Most groups will let you sell directly to members after the presentation.

More on Libraries. There are more than 1000,000 libraries in the United States, Ranging from academic to public, and they buy a lot of books. Your title becomes a permanent advertisement when sitting on their shelves. Many

Offical Contact Pages: Creating a Demand

public libraries have an events coordinator or "Friends of the Library" groups who organize author and fundraising activities. Look to local libraries for generating publicity and reviews through signings, workshops and lectures. Libraries typical purchase books through wholesalers, and occasionally direct from the publisher.

Write an Article. Since you know more about your topic than most people, share your knowledge and publicize your book at the same time. Many magazines, trade journals, newspapers and newsletters welcome newsworthy articles.

Fundraisers. Most groups, schools and organizations re looking for ways to generate revenues. If there is a good fir, donate a percentage of your book sales to their cause in exchange for selling and endorsing your book.

Premiums & Incentives. Many businesses offer premiums as incentives to their employees and customers. Why shouldn't that premium be your book? See the Thomas Register of their Regional directory in the library for a list of companies and products to find a tie-in.

Book Trade Shows. The primary purpose of a regional or national book trade show is to introduce new titles to the trade. You may display your new book on your own, or pay someone else to do so. Bookstore owners who attend will browse and make seasonal buying decisions; this is an ideal opportunity to win shelf in their stores.

Trade Shows and Conventions. Selling your book at a trade show or convention can be a profitable experience. Assembled in one place is a high concentration of potential buyers. This becomes a great place to make valuable contacts and get exposure to an industry. Use the *Encyclopedia of Associations* in the library to find our what groups are holding meetings or conventions in your vicinity. The *Chamber of Commerce* and a city's *Convention Centers* are also helpful contacts.

Book, Art & Street Fairs. Sponsors promote to the general public to a niche group of people and thus are a great forum for showing and selling your book direct. Calculate your break-even point before paying for space. Sharing space with another author will reduce your costs.

Book Awards & Contests. An award or a nomination can be a profitable and satisfying experience, generating free publicity for your book. Submit your title to the various organizations that offer such contests. See the *Literary Market Place* or *Writer's Market* in the library for listings.

The Media. Print and electronic media (newspapers, magazines, radio and television) are under pressure to fill space or time with news. Media exposure gives an author expert status that even the largest advertising budget can't touch. The media needs you as much as you need them. For example, unsolicited news releases occupy nearly 20% of editorial space. Locally, you and your book are news and should have an edge to get air time or print space. See *The Directory of Publications* and *Broadcast Media* in the library. The following sell ways to reach the national media:

Radio TV Interview Report
Bradley Communications
135 E. Plumstead Ave.
Lansdowne, PA 1950
(800) 989-1400
www.rtir.com

Talk Show Selects
Broadcast Interviews Source
2233 Wisconsin Ave NW
#301
Washington, DC 20007
(800) 932-7266
www.yearbooknews.com

Radio. Radio is your most accessible form of publicity. If you enjoy talking about your book, you will enjoy radio interviews. More than 750 radio talk shows in the country re looking for interesting guests. Most conduct interviews over the phone, which means you don't have to leave your home. Some will even tape an interview to be aired at a future date. Phone the Program Director of Producer of the station and say: *"I have a story that will be of interest to your audience"*. Be prepared to quickly explain why your message will be important to their listeners. Make an interview with you sound appealing. Start off by interviewing on smaller

Offical Contact Pages: Creating a Demand

stations you contact, the more interviews you will get. Assume the interviewer has not read your book. This is the case more often than not, and he will rely on the Media Kit you send him in advance. Phone bookstores in the stations broadcast area before your radio interview to ensure they have you book in stock. See *The American Book Trade Directory* in the library for national bookstore listings.

Newspapers. Perhaps your book can address a lifestyle, business, gardening, travel or cooking issue. Send a news release and cover letter to the appropriate editor, with a possible story angle. If your book relates to problem that just hit the headlines, get on the phone and try to secure an interview. More than 900 daily and weekly newspapers throughout the country are searching for news.

Television. Wouldn't be ideal if the major national talk show hosts invited you to discuss your book on their shows? When getting started, it is more realistic to be a guest on a local afternoon news program not a TV magazine talk show. Contact the show's producer with your story, convincing him of a possible angle for the show. Local cable access stations offer a great place to practice live interviews. TV leaves a powerful impression in the viewer's mind and can translate into an explosion of book sales.

Magazines. Thousands of magazines cater to every audience you can imagine. Offer reprints of a portion of you book in exchange for a free ad and / or a by-line at the end of your article. Do not neglect local and regional publications as they may be more accommodating to local authors. See *Standard Periodical Directory* at the public library for a complete listing of national magazines and their focus.

Word-of Mouth. Word-of-mouth can be the fastest and most efficient form of free advertising. This happens when people have heard, seen, bought or read your book and told others about it. The more books in people's hands, the better the chance they will spread the word. Anything you can do to get people talking about your book will generate interest and sales. Media appearances and favorable reviews all contribute to word-of-mouth advertising.

Advertising. After you have exhausted all other means of publicity, turn to paid advertising. Advertising comes in many forms, although the intent is always the same: to motivate a desired response. This is done by developing an ad that gains the readers' favorable attention holds it long enough to get the intended message across and then motivates a pre determined action. When designing an ad, talk about the readers' interest, as they are interested in what the book will do for them. Two general rules of advertising success are timing and repetition.

Space Advertising. Space advertising involves placing an advertisement or insert in newspapers, catalogs, newsletters, books, magazines, or any supplement which targets you audience. Orders are placed by the customer by mail or calling a toll-free number, and then shipped by you or your fulfillment service. At the reference desk in the public library see:

Standard Rate and Data Lists magazines, periodicals, demographics and their advertising rates.

Standard Periodical Directory: Directory of national magazines

Directory of Publications & Broadcast Media: List daily and weekly newspapers in the U.S.

Classified Ads. This is one of the least expensive forms of advertising. Classifieds ads are best used to compile a good mailing list or to test market the pull of an ad instead of selling books. Offer free information in return for a self-addressed, stamped enveloped (SASE). Follow this up by sending an article, flyer, brochure or promotional material that encourages a purchase. A mailing list complied from classified response could yield high numbers of orders. Code your ads to keep track of what works and what doesn't.

Direct Mail Advertising. It is easier to sell books by direct mail if you can accurately identify and locate your audience or niche. Direct mail is quick to produce. With the

Offical Contact Pages: Creating a Demand

correct list, offer, and sales copy, direct mail can be a profitable way to reach your audience. Ask yourself: Is my product suitable to direct mail? Where can I advertise? Am I prepared to handle the incoming mail response or should I use a fulfillment service? To determine the profitability of using direct mail, keep in mind that a 0-5% response rate is common. Associations and magazines generally rent the mailing list of their membership or subscribers. See *Encyclopedia of Associations* and *Standard Periodical Directory* in the library.

NOTE: *Before making a sizable investment in advertising, start small to test the effectiveness of your message. This way you can adjust your message until it yields the best results.*

Check into the legal regulations of mail order advertising in your state to follow the guidelines set forth by law. Write the FTC and phone your State's Attorney General's office and request information about complying with those regulations:

Federal Trade Commission (FTC)
Pennsylvania Ave & 6th ST NW
Washington DC 20580
www.ftc.gov

Co-op mailing is combining your mailer with someone else's and then sharing the expenses. This reduces your mailing costs, but dilutes you message. Co-op with someone whose product is compatible with yours; to reduce competing or conflicting messages.

Mailing Lists. Below are mailing list mangers and brokers who specialize in renting targeted lists and address labels to book publishers. Request list types and pricing.

American Booksellers Assoc.
828 S Broadway
Tarrytown, NY 10591
(800) 637-0037
www.bookweb.org

Cahners Business lists
1350 E. Touhy AVE.
Des Plaines, IL 60018
(800) 323-4958
www.cahners.com

Para-Lists by Poynter
Box 8206
Santa Barbara, CA 93118
(800) 727-2782
www.parapublishing.com

Triplex
781 Lincoln Ave. Ste. 170
San Rafael, CA 94901
(415) 256-1600
www.tdmc.com

HR Direct
508 N. Second ST
Fairfield, IA 52556
(641) 472-7188
www.hrdirect.net

American Business Lists
5711 S. 86th Cr
Omaha, NE 68127
(800) 336-8349
www.infousa.com

Twin Peaks Mailing Lists
Box 129
Vancouver, WA 98666
(360) 694-2462
www.pacifer.com/~twinpeak/press

AllMedia Inc.
6900 Dallas Parkway, Ste. 750
Plano, TX 75024
(800) 466-4061
www.allmediainc.com

Ioma
3 Park Avenue 30th Fl
New York, NY 10016
(212) 244-0360
www.institutelists.com

American List Council (ALC)
4300 Rte 1
CN-5219
Princeton, NJ 08543
(609) 580-2800
www.amlist.com

Open Horizons
POB 205
Fairfield, IA 52556
(800) 796-6130

The Internet

    The World Wide Web on the Internet is the most important new communication medium since TV. It is a rapidly growing marketplace for the sale of books. The following are common ways to sell books using the Internet.
    Web Site. A web site is essentially a storefront on the World Wide Web that people can visit via computers. It

Offical Contact Pages: Creating a Demand

acts as an introduction, to you, your book(s) and your publishing venture using a collection of information presented in words, sounds, and images. A Web site can include your promotional programs, such as: new book announcements, news release, book review, schedule of author appearances, excerpts, a graphic of a book's cover, ordering information and even links to services at other Web locations. When people visit your site, they may order, print or request additional information on your products or services. See the *Yellow Pages* under "Internet Service Providers" and inquire about the cost and requirements to develop a web site. The following companies specialize in the development of Web Sites for book publishers.

Promoting Your Web Site. Establishing an Internet presence is not enough. An active promotional strategy to attract people to your site is essential. To make the most of this technology, an effective strategy might include:

Search Engines and Directories. Let the world know your site exists. An important way is to register your site in the online indexes that most people use to find things on the Web.

Alta Vista	www.altavista.com
Excite	www.excite.com
Hot Bot	www.hotbot.com
Infoseek	www.infoseek.com
Lycos	www.lycos.com
Webcrawler	www.webcrawler.com
Yahoo	www.yahoo.com
MammaMetasearch	www.mamma.com
Dogpile Web	www.dogpile.com
Search.com	www.search.com
AllSearchEngines.com	www.allsearchengines.com
MSN	www.search.msn.com
AlltheWeb.com	www.alltheweb.com
Ask.com	www.ask.com
Search Engine Guide	www.searchengineguide.com
Google	www.google.com

For a ranking of the top 100 places to be listed and assistance in submitting your site to them, visit John Audettes WebStop 100 at: www.mmgco.com/top100.html.

Reciprocal Links. Exchanging links with other sites that attract the same audience is one of the most effective ways to promote your site and books. Send an email requesting an exchange. It's often easier to first establish a link to other sites, then ask for a link to yours.

Participating in Newsgroups. Newsgroups are another way people with similar interests get together. When visiting a newsgroup, offer help in your area of expertise. Simply post an informative article and send to any discussion group (newsgroup) or bulletin board (BBS) catering to your market niche saying that you would be glad to answer questions about your subject of expertise. Once you have established familiarity and trust, people will seek your advice. Be mindful of online etiquette when promoting your book. Check the FAQs (frequently asked questions), which are usually posted within each discussion/newsgroup, for do's and don'ts. Newsgroup subject directories can be found at: www.reference.com and www.dejanews.com.

Book Marketing Contacts on the Internet.

- **Book Marketing On-Line.** Receive a free weekly book marketing update by sending an e-mail to: Majordomo@bookzone.com and type in the message area: subscribe bmu.

- **Publishers Marketing Association's Mailing List.** This is a forum publishers who share ideas and answer questions for list members. To join, send an e-mail to: listserv@hslc.org and type in the message area SUBSCRIBE PMA-L along with you name.

- **Self-Publishing Resource Center by Wise Owl Books.** Useful articles. FAQs and a valuable links page. www.wiseowlbooks.com/publish

Shipping Books

Shipping & Mailing Books. When shipping pallets of books, use national trucking lines listed in the phone book. They base their rates on shipping location, weight, and freight class. Paperback books have a different and less expensive freight class than the standard book class rate (class 60 versus 65 respectively). UPS ground offers a fine service for smaller quantities and offers a pick-up service to contracted customers. Single copies can be mailed most economically through the Postal Service at **Book Rate**. The Post Office also offers **Priority Mail** at a bargain price compared to the overnight express service, if an extra day or two delay won't make a difference. Shipping expenses add up quickly. Managing postage and shipping costs is a good business practice. When mailing large quantities on a daily basis, the phone book lists mailing services which specialize in sending bulk quantities.

Discount Schedule and Policy. Set a discount policy from the very start that is simple, clear and in writing so there is no misunderstanding. It is a requirement by the FTC that any discount you offer one type of dealer must be given to others who buy the same quantity. Your terms may differ when dealing with conventional channels of distribution as many work on a consignment basis only. Create a separate sheet of terms and discounts for Wholesalers, Bookstores and Special Direct Sales (*alternative channels of distribution*) as standard discounts and terms differ for each. Include in your Terms and Conditions statement:

- Who pays the shipping and from where
- Breakdown of the quantity discount schedule
- Payment terms
- How to establish credit with you
- Return policy (if any)

➢ Special services such as *dropshipping* & S.T.O.P.'s

➢ (**S**ingle **T**itle **O**rder **P**lans *is used by bookstores to order from publishers.*)

    A Final Note. Publishing and promoting your own book can be an enriching experience. At times things will not run smoothly, and you will ask yourself: "What did I get myself into?" Some discouragement can be expected. Meet other self-published authors in your area to pool resources and share experiences. This can be a source of encouragement, a way to shorten learning time and an opportunity to combine promotional efforts. Welcome to the exciting world of publishing, and . . . **Good Luck!**

APPENDIX

1. 5 Major Publisher's

AOL TIME WARNER BOOK GROUP
3 Center Plaza Boston, MA 02108
(617) 227-0730
www.twbookmark.com

Time Warner Book Group
Time and Life Building
1271 Avenue of the Americas
New York, NY 10020
212-522-7200

Warner Faith
10 Cadillac Dr. Ste. 220 Brentwood, TN 37027
615-221-0996

Warner Aspect
Mysterious Press
Warner Twelve
Time Warner Audio Book

Little, Brown & Company Adult Trade Books

Back Bay BooksBulfinch Press

Little Brown & Company Children's Publishing

Megan Tingley Books

HARPERCOLLINS PUBLISHING GROUPS
HarperCollins Publishers
10 East 53rd St. New York, NY 10022
(212) 207-7000

ww w harperc ollins.com
www.harperc hildrens.com
www.ha rperteen.com
www.h arperacademic.c om
www.harpe rteacher.com
www.harpertools.com

Harper Collins General Books Group
Amistad Press
Avon
Dark Alley
Ecco Press
Eos
Fourth Estate
HarperAudio/Caedmon
HarperCollins
Harper Entertainment
Harper Large Print
Harper Resource
Harper San Francisco
Harper Torch
PerfectBound
Rayo
ReganBooks
William Morrow

HarperCollins Children's
Harper Collins Children's Book Group1350 Avenue of the AmericasNew York, NY 70019
212-261-6500
www.harperchildrens.com

Amistad
Avon
Eos/ Harper Teen
Greenwillow Books
HarperCollins Childrens's Books
Harper Festival
Harper Kids Entertainment
Harper Tempest/ Harper Teen
Harper Trophy
Joanna Cotler Books

Offical Contact Pages: Appendix 5 Major Publishers

Julie Andrews Collection
Katherine Tegen Books
Laura Geringer Books
Rayo

HOLTZBRINCK PUBLISHERS (Germany)
Holtzbrinck Publishers
175 Fifth Ave.New York, NY 10010
(646) 307-5151
www.holtzbrinckus.com

Bedford
33 Irving PlaceNew York, NY 10003
212-375-7000

75 Arlington St.Boston, MA 02116
617-399-4000
www.bedfordstmartins.com

Farrar, Straus and Giroux
19 Union Square WestNew York, NY 10003
212-741-6900
www.fsgbooks.com

Audio Renaissance
Audio Renaissance

Farrar, Straus & Giroux
North Point Press
Hill and Wang
Faber and Faber

Henry Holt
Henry Holt Trade
Metropolitan Books
Times Books
Owl Books
Henry Holt for Young Readers

Palgrave Macmillan
Palgrave Macmillan

Picador
Picador USA

Roaring Brook Press
Roaring Brook Press

St. Martin's Press
175 Fifth Avenue New York, NY 100100
212-674-5151
www.stmartins.com

Griffin
Minotaur
St. Martin's Press Paperbacks
Let's Go
Thomas Dunne Books
Truman Talley Books

Scientific American
Scientific American
Scientific American Mind

Tor/Forge
Tor/Forge

St. Martin's Reference Group
Golden Guides and Goldenfield Guides

Griffin Trade Paperbacks
Encarta
Forge Books
Orb Books
Worth

W.H. Freeman
41 Madison Ave. 37th Fl New York, NY 10010
212-578-9400

PENGUIN GROUP (USA) INC.
375 Hudson St. New York, NY 10014
us.penguingroup.com
212-366-2000

Offical Contact Pages: Appendix 5 Major Publishers

Adult Division
Ace
Alpha
Avery
Berkley Books Group
Chamberlin Bros.
Dutton
Gotham Books
Putnam
HPBooks
Hudson Street Press
Jeremy P. Tarcher
Jove
Penguin Press
Perigee Books
Plume
Portfolio
Riverhead Books
Sentinel
Viking

Young Readers Division
Dial Books for Young Readers
Dutton Children's Books (Dutton, Grosset and Dunlap)
Firebird
Frederick Warne
Putnam
Grosset & Dunlap
Philomel
Price Stern Sloan
Puffin Books
Speak
Viking Children's Books

G.P. Putnam's Sons Books for Young Readers

RANDOM PUBLISHING GROUP
1745 BroadwayNew York, NY 10019
(212) 782-9000 Fax: (212) 572-6066
www.randomhouse.com

Ballantine Publishing Group
Kids@random
Knopf Publishing Group
Bantam Dell Publishing Group
Everyman's Library

Random House Trade Publishing Group
Random House Trade Books
Villard Books
St. River's Row
The Modern Library
Presidio Press

Random House Information Group
Foder's Travel Publications
House of Collections
Living Language
Princeton Review
Random House Espanol
Random House Puzzles and GamesThe Princeton ReviewRandom House Reference Publishing

Bantam Dell Publishing Group
Bantam
Delacorte Press
Dell
Delta
The Dial Press
Fanfare
IslandS
pectra

The Crown Publishing Group
Clarkson Potter/ Publishers Crown Business
Harmony Books
Shaye Areheart Books
Three Rivers Press
Crown Books
Crown Forum

Offical Contact Pages: Appendix 5 Major Publishers

The Doubleday Broadway Publishing Group
Broadway Books
Currency
DoubleDay
Doubleday Religious Publishing
Main Street Books
Nan A.Talese
Harlem Moon

SIMON & SCHUSTER INC.
1230 Avenue of the Americas New York, NY 10020
(212) 698-7000 (800) 223-2336
www.simonsays.com
consumer.customerservice@simonandschuster.com

Simon & Schuster Adult Publishing
Atria Books
Kaplan
Pocket Books
Scribner
Simon & Schuster
Free Press
Touchstone
MTV Books

Simon & Schuster Audio
Pimsleur
Simon & Schuster Sound Ideas
Simon & Schuster Audioworks

Simon & Schuster Children's Publishing
Aladdin Paperbacks
Atheneum Books for Young Readers
Little Simon
Little Simon Inspirations
Margaret K. McElderry Books
Simon & Schuster Books for Young Readers
Simon Pulse
Simon Spotlight
www.adibooks.com

2. BOOK PRINTERS

#1 Printers – CS Young, Inc.
8201 Greensboro Dr, Ste. 1000
McLean, VA 22102

A&A Printing, Inc (POD)
6103 Johns Rd.
Tampa, FL 33634
(813) 886-0065
(866) 886-0065
www.printshopcentral.com

ACE Printing & Graphics
2220 Midland Ave.
Toronto, ON M1P 3E6
(Canada)
416-292-9299
www.aceprintingca.com

Action Printing
N6637 Rolling Meadows Dr.
Fond du Lac, WI 54937
(800) 472-0337
www.actionprinting.com

Adibooks.com (POD)
181 Industrial Ave.
Lowell, MA 01852
(978) 458-2345
www.adibooks.com

ADR BookPrint
2012 E. Northern Ave
Wichita, KS 67216
(800) 767-6066
www.adrbookprint.com

Advanced Digital Copies, Inc.
13435 S.E. 128th St Ste. 105
Miami, FL 33186
(305) 969-0052

Affordable Words
POB 1678
Snellville, GA 30078
(877) 425-2985
(770) 601-5208
www.affordablewords.com

Alexander's Print Advantage (POD)
245 South 1060 West
Lindon, UT 84042
(800) 574-8666
www.alexanders.com

All-American Printing Services (POD)
1130 Industrial Ave, Ste 12
Petaluma, CA 94952
(707) 762-2500 ext. 116
(800) 210 AAPS
www.allamericanprinting.com

Allen ASA W Baby Books
748 South Decatur St.
Montgomery, AL 36104
(334) 264-4581
www.alabamaprinters.com

Alphagraphics of Gwinnett
3075 Breckinridge Blv. Ste. 445
Duluth, GA 30096
(770) 279-8882
(877) 298-4165
www.gwinnett433.alphagraphics.com

Offical Contact Pages: Appendix Book Printers

Alpha Graphics Printshops
2159 Rocky Ridge Rd. Ste. 107
Birmingham, AL 35216
(205) 979-2373
www.us448.alphagraphics.com

Ames On- Demand (POD)
30 Dane St.
Somerville, MA 02143
(617) 776-3360 ext. 1136 or 1138
www.amesondemand.com

Amica International Inc.
844 Industry Dr.
Seattle, WA 98188
(800) 622-9256
www.amicaint.com

Angus Consulting, Inc.
PMB 249
1514 Skyland Blv.
Tuscaloosa, AL 35405
(205) 507-4633
www.angusconsulting.com

Area Printing & Design
POB 767053
Roswell, GA 30076
(678) 325-2732
(877) 268-9110
www.areaprinting.com

Arvato Services
28210 North Avenue Stanford
Valencia, CA 91355
(800) 223-1478 ext. 4592
www.arvatousa.com

Asia Pacific Offset Inc.
1332 Corcoran St. N.W. #6
Washington, D.C. 20009
(800) 756-4344
(202) 462-5436
www.asiapacificoffset.com

AsianPrinting.com
969G Edgewater Blvd. #717
Foster City, CA 94404
(650) 573-9268
www.asianprinting.com

Automated Graphics Systems
4590 Graphics Dr.
White Plains, MD 20695
(800) 678-8760
www.ags.com

Axess Purchasing Solutions (POD)
POD Division
POB 500835
Atlanta, GA 31150
(770) 521-9939

Bang Printing
1473 Hwy 18 E
POB 587
Brainerd, MN 56401
www.bangprinting.com

Bay Port Press
645- D Marsat Ct.
Chula Vista, CA 91911
(800) 994-7737
(619) 429-0100

Berryville Graphics (POD)
Bertelsmann Printing & Manufacturing
25 Jack Enders Blvd.
Berryville, VA 22611
(800) 382-7249
www.bvgraphics.com

Bethany Press
6820 W. 115th St.
Bloomington, MN 55438
(952) 914-7400
www.bethanypress.com

BG Enterprises
234 Pine Cone Trail
Ormond Beach, FL 32174
(904) 673-7993
www.bgenterprises.net

Blitzprint (POD)
#3 1235 Sixty-Fourth Ave. SE
Calgary, Alberta T2J 2Jy (Canada)
(866) 479-3248
(403)-253-4460
www.blitzprint.com

BooksJustBooks.com
51 East 42nd St. Ste. 1202
New York, NY 10017
(800) 621-2556
www.booksjustbooks.com

BookSurge, LLC (POD)
5341 Dorchester Rd. Ste 16
North Charleston, SC 29418
(866) 308-6235 ext. 123
www.booksurgepublishing.com
www.booksurgepublisherservices.com

BooksOnDemand.com (POD)
Gene Whitford
540 Business park Cir.
Stoughton, WI 53589
(608-205-9555

Boyd Printing Company, Inc.
49 Sheridan Avenue
Albany, New York 12210
(800) 877-2693
www.boydprinting.com

Braceland
7625 Suffolk Ave.
Philadelphia, PA 19153
(215) 492-0200
(800) 338-1280
www.braceland.com

Brenner Printing
1234 Triplett
San Antonio, TX 78216
(210) 349-4024
www.brennerprinting.com

C&M Press (POD)
4825 Nome St.
Denver, CO 80239
(303) 375-9922
www.cmpress.com

Codra Enterprises Inc.
5912 Bolsa Ave. #200
Huntington Beach, CA 92649
(714) 891-5652 ext. 32
www.codra.com

ColorCentric Corp. (POD)
10 Carlson Rd.
Rochester, NY 14610

Offical Contact Pages: Appendix Book Printers

(585) 288-1240
www.colorcentriccorp.com
Color House Graphics (POD)
3505 Eastern Ave.
Grand Rapids, MI 49508
(616) 241-1916
www.colorhousegraphics.com

Commonwealth Litho
310 S. Nina Dr.
Mesa, AZ 85210
(480) 649-6494

Consolidated Reprographics
Services (POD)
31 Musick Ave.
Irvine, CA 92618
(949)-588-3839
www.consrepro.com

Copy Concepts, Inc.
8080 Tristar Dr. Ste. 112
Irving, TX 75063
(800) 644-2111
www.copcon.com

Corley Printing Company
3777 Rider Trail South
St. Louis. MO 63045
(314) 739-3777
Atlanta Sales Office

Corley Printing Company
3020 Roswell Rd. #200
Marietta, GA 30062
(770) 321-1223
www.corleyprinting.com

The Country Press, Inc.
(POD)
1 Commercial Dr.
Lakeville, MA 02347

(508) 947-4485
www.countrypressinc.com
Covington Group
4050 Pennsylvania Ste. 230
Kansa City, MO 64111
(816) 753-1988
www.covingtongroup.net

Crane Duplicating (POD)
POB 1600
Harwich, MA 02645
(508) 760-1601
www.craneduplicating.com

Creative Printing USA, Inc.
Raritan Professional Building
324 Raritan Ave. Ste. 110
Highland Park, NJ 08904
(732) 572-5185

CS Graphics USA inc.
8969 Lake Ct.
Granite Bay, CA 95746
916-791-9066
www.ourworld.compuserve.com/homepages/csgraphics

Cushing Malloy, Inc.
POB 8632
1350 N. Main St.
Ann Arbor, MI 48107
(888) 295-7244
www.cushing-malloy.com

Dallas Offset
2100 Panoramic Cir.
POB 223664
Dallas, TX 75212
(214) 630-8741
www.dallasoffset.com

Darby Printing Company
6215 Purdure Dr.
Atlanta, GA 30336
(800) 241-5292
www.darbyprinting.com

Data Reproductions Corp.
4545 Glenmeade Ln.
Auburn Hills, MI 48326
(248) 371-3700
(800) 242-3114
www.datapro.com

Delta Printing Solutions
28210 N. Ave. Stanford
Valencia, CA 91355
(800) 32- DELTA
www.deltaprintingsolutions.com

Des Plaines Publishing Company
1000 Executive Way
Des Plaines, IL 60018
(800) 283-1776
www.dppc.com

Diamond Publications
14061 Airport Blv.
Mobile, AL 36608
(251) 776-5717

Dickinson Press Inc.
5100 33rd St. SE
Grand Rapids, MI 49512
(616) 957-5100
www.dickinsonpress.com

DiYA USA
219 Loon Ct.
Foster City, CA 94404

(650) 888-0302

Don Yeatts
318 West Hornbeam Dr.
Longwood, FL 32779
(407-230-4374

Downtown Printing Center
46 Paterson St.
New Brunswick, NJ 08901
(732) 246-7990
www.downtownprinting.com

EBSCO Media, Publications Dept.
801 – 5th Ave. South
Birmingham, AL 35233
(800) 765-0852
www.ebscomedia.com

Eardmans Printing Company
231 Jefferson SE
Grand Rapids, MI 49503
(616) 451-0763
www.eerdmansprinting.com

Elite Printing International Company, Ltd.
13001 Ramona Blv. Ste. C
Irwindale, CA 91706
(626) 337-5300
eliteprinter@cs.com

Emporium of Imagination
102 N Washington St.
Magnolia, AR 71753
(870) 901-6455
www.emporiausa.com

Faith Printing Co.
4210 Locust Hill Rd.

Offical Contact Pages: Appendix Book Printers

Taylors, SC 29687
(864) 895-3822
Fidlar Doubleday (POD)
4570 Commercial Ave. Ste. A
Portage, MI 49002
(800) 248-0888
www.fidlardoubleday.com

FolgerGraphics, Inc.
2339 Davis Ave.
Hayward, CA 94545
(510) 887-5656
www.folgergraphics.com

Franklin Printing
POB 184
Meadville, MS 39653
(601) 384-2366

Friesens Corporation
Book Division
One Printers Way
Altona, Manitoba R0G 0B
(Canada)
(204-324-6401
www.friesens.com

G-A Printers
731 Grogan St.
Lavonia, GA 30553
(706) 356-1319

Genesis Publishing Co.
36 Steeple View Dr.
Atkinson, NH 03811

Georgia International
1565 Holmesville Rd.
Jesup, GA 31545
(912) 427-3824

G&H Soho Inc. (POD)
117 Grand St.

Hoboken, NJ 07030
(201) 216-9400
www.ghsoho.com

GB Printing Enterprises, Inc.
(POD)
510 Heron Dr. Ste. 204
Logan Township, NJ 08085
(856) 241-2790
www.gbprint.com

Graphic Arts Unlimited
599 Nye Ave.
Irvington, NJ 07111
(973) 371-1717
www.graphicartsunlimited.com

The Gray Printing Co.
401 E. North St.
Fostoria, Ohio 44830
(419) 435-6638
www.grayprinting.com

Green Button Inc. (POD)
133 Oxford St.
Hanover Township, PA
18706
(570) 704-0334
www.greenbuttoninc.com

Global Impressions
3494 Camino Tassajara Ste. 311
Danville, CA 94506
(925) 736-6740

Global Interprint
589 Mendocino Ave.
Santa Rosa, CA 95401
(707) 545-1220
www.globalinterprint.com

Godar & Hossenlopp Printing Company
151 Mitchell Ave.
S. San Francisco, CA 94080
(415) 970-0155

Gorham Printing (POD)
334 Harris Rd.
Rochester, WA 98579
(800) 837-0970
www.gorhamprinting.com

Graphics International
969G Edgewater Blv. St 717
Foster City, CA 94404
(650) 573-9268
www.asianprinting.com

Great Impressions Printing & Graphics
444 W. Mockingbird LN
Dallas, TX 75247
(214) 631-2665

Hagerswtown Bookbinding and Printing (POD)
952 Frederick St.
Hagerstown, MD 21740
(800) 638-3508
www.hdp.com

Hart Graphics
10228 Technology Dr.
Knoxville, TN 37932
(865)-675-1600
www.hartgraphics.com

Hollandays Publishing
32 North Main St.
Dayton, OH 45402
(937) 898-2520

www.hollandays.net
Houston Datum (POD)
8885 Monroe
Houston, TX 77061
(713) 944-4600
www.houstondatum.com/html/digital print.html

Huron Vally Printing & Imaging
4557 Washtenaw Ave.
Ann Arbor, MI 48108
(734) 971-1700
www.hvpi.com

Imago Sales (USA)
17 N. Loomis ST #4A
Chicago, IL 60607
(312) 829-4051
imagousa@imagousa.com

Impressions Unlimited (POD)
2300 Windsor Ct. Unit C
Addison, IL 60101
(630) 705-6464
www.impressionsunltd.com

Inland Press / Inland Book
W141 N9450 Fountain Blv.
Menoomonee Falls, WI 53051
(800) 552-2235
www.inlandbook.com

Instantpublisher.com (POD)
(subsidiary of Fundcraft Publishing, Inc.)
POB 985
Collierville, TN 38027
www.instantpublisher.com

Offical Contact Pages: Appendix Book Printers

Jaguar Advanced Graphics
198 Grumman Rd. West
Bethpage, NY 11714
(516) 512-1400
(800) 972-9550
www.jaguargraphics.com

Jinno International Company
2235 Sheppard Ave. East #903
Willowdale, ON M2J 5B5 (Canada)
(416) 491-8811

Jostens Commercial Publications
Jostens Inc. Corporate Headquarters
5501 Norman Center Dr.
Minneapolis, MN 55437
www.jostens.com

Keystone Digital Press (POD)
210 Carter Dr.
West Chester, PA 19382
(610) 344-9118
www.kdpress.com

Kirby Lithographic Co., Inc.
2900 South Eads St.
Arlington, VA 22202
(800) 932-3594
www.kirbylitho.com

Kimco On Demand Printers (POD)
4120 Brighton Blv. Ste A-21
Denver, CO 80216
(888) 345-4626
(303) 295-1172

kimcoprinting@qwest.net
King Printing Co. Inc.(POD)
181 Industrial Ave. E
Lowell, MA 01852
www.kingprinting.com

Kwong Fat Offset Printing, Ltd.
3926 Valrica Grove Dr.
Valrico, FL 33594
(813) 657-5874

The Lehigh Press
7001 North Park Dr.
Pennsauken, NJ
(856) 665-5200
www.lehigh-press.com

Lewis Creative Technologies
900 West Leigh St.
Richmond, VA 23261
www.lewisct.com

Lightning Press Printing Group
140 Furler St.
Totowa, NJ 07512
(973) 890-4422
www.lightning-press.com

Lithocolor Press
9825 W. Roosevelt Rd.
Westchester, IL 60154
(708) 345-5530
www.lithocolor.com

Marrakech Express Inc.
720 Wesley Ave.
Tarpon Springs, FL 34689
(800) 940-6566
print@marrak.com

Mccormick's Bindery
5815 Magnolia Ave.
Pennsauken, NJ 08109
(856) 663-8035

Media Lithographics, Inc.
(POD)
6080 Triangle Dr.
City of Commerce, CA 90040
www.medialitho.com

Medius Corp. (POD)
1103 Montague Ct.
Milpitas, CA 94035
(408) 519-5000
www.mediuscorp.com

Mercury Print Productions
(POD)
50 Holleder Parkway
Rochester, NY 14615
(585) 458-7900
www.mercuryprint.com

Milanostampa New
Interlitho USA
299 Broadway Ste. 901
New York, NY 10007
(212) 964-2430
www.milanostampa.com

Minder International
1411 W. 190th St. Ste. 110
Gardena, CA 90248
(310) 851-5600
www.mdr.com

Minuteman Press
2822 S. Dixie Hwy.
West Palm Beach, FL 33405
(866) 272-0863
(561) 655-5355
www.minutemanpress.com

M.O.M Printing
300 Parkdale Ave.
Ottawa, Ontario K1Y 1G2
(613) 729-4303
(800) 267-9955
sales@momgroup.com

Monument Press
Memphis, TN 38117
(901) 328-7206

MOPC Inc.
579 S. State College Blvd.
Fullerton, CA 92831
(714) 871-5560

Mosaic Press LLC
3543 Indian Creek Rd. Ste. A
Happy Camp, CA 96039
mosaic@sisqtel.net

NetPub Corp. (POD)
2 Neptune Rd.
Poughkeepsie, NY 12601
(800) 724-1100
www.netpub.net

Network Printers
1010 S. 70th St.
Milwaukee, WI 53214
(414) 443-0530
www.network-printers.com/index.asp

Newark Trade Digital Graphics
177 Oakwood Ave.
Orange, NJ 07050
(973) 674-3727

Offical Contact Pages: Appendix Book Printers

www.newarktrade.com
Nu-Tec Litho
370 San Aleso Ave.
Sunnyvale, CA 94083
www.nu-tec. Com

Odyssey Press Inc. (POD)
22 Nadeau Dr. POB 7307
Gonic, NH 03839
(603) 749-4433
www.odysseypress.com

Omega Bindery
3773 Silver Star Rd.
Orlando, FL 32808
(407) 294-9230
omegabind@mailcity.com

On-Demand Technologies, Inc. (POD)
2220 Tomlynn Street
Richmond, VA 23230
(804) 359-4087
www.on-demandtech.com

Overseas Printing Corp.
99 The Embarcadero
San Francisco, CA 94105
(415) 835-9999

Pacific Rim International Printing
11726 San Vicente Blv. Ste. 280
Los Angeles, CA 90049
(800) 952-6567
www.pacrim-intl.com

Palace Press, International
180 Varick St. 10th Fl
New York, NY 10014
(212) 462-2622

www.palacepress.com
Papergraphics
4 John Tyler St.
Merrick, NH 03054
(603) 880-1835
www.papergraphics.biz

Patterson Printing
1550 Territorial Rd.
Benton Harbor, MI 49022
(800) 848-8826 ext. 542
www.patterson-printing.com

Phillips Brothers
1555 W. Jefferson
POB 580
Springfield, IL 62705
(800) 637-9327
www.pbpweb.com

Phoenix Color
540 Western Maryland Pkwy
Hagertown, MD 21740
(800) 632-4111
www.phoenixcolor.com

Pinnacle Press
2662 Metro Blv.
St. Louis, MO 63043
(800) 760-0010
www.pinnaclepress.com

P.O.D. Wholesale (POD)
519 W. Lancaster Ave.
Haverford, PA 19041
(610) 520-2500
www.podwholesale.com

Prime Mover (POD)
9999 Muirlands Blv.
Irvine, CA 92618
(949) 251-8771

www.primemover.net
Print Masters
2507 South Thompson St. 10
Springdale, AR 72764
(888) 927-4224
www.printmasters2000.com

The Printing Council
17320 Prairie St
Northridge, CA 91325
(877) 632-2276
www.printingcouncil.com

The Printing House
Publication Specialists
540 Business Park Cir.
Stoughton, WI 53589
(800) 873-8990
www.printinghouseinc.com

Printing Industry Exchange, LLC
POB 2238
Ashburn, VA 20146-2238
(703) 631-4533
www.PrintIndustry.com

Progressive Printing
6700 Springfield Center Dr.
Springfield, VA 22150
(703) 719-0050
www.progressiveprinting.org

Publisher's Graphics, LLC
290 Gerzevske Ln.
Carol Stream, IL 60188
(888) 404-3769
www.pubgraphics.com

Quebecor World
340 Pemberwick Rd.
Greenwich, CT 06831

(203) 532-4200
www.quebecorworld.com

Quinn Woodbine
419 Park Aven S. Ste. 1201
New York, NY 10016
(212) 8890552
www.quinnwoodbine.com

R&B Bindery
2250 Sherman Ave.
Pennsauken, NJ
(856) 662-7005

R.J. Comminications
51 East 42nd St. Ste. 1202
New York, NY 10017
(800) 621-2556
www.rjcom.com

Regent Publishing Services
367 E. Napa St.
Sonoma, CA 95476
regentso@concentric.net

Robinson Graphics Inc.
217 Connell St.
Goodlettsville, TN 37072
(615) 859-4875

Sentinel Printing Co. Inc.
250 Highway 10 North
St. Cloud, MN 56304
(800) 450-6434
(320) 251-6434
www.sentinelprinting.com

Sharp Offset Printing &
Academy Books
10 Cleveland Ave.
POB 757
Rutland, Vermont 05701

Offical Contact Pages: Appendix Book Printers

(800) 773-9194
www.sharpoffsetprinting.com

Sheridan Printing
1425 Third Ave
Alpha, NJ 08865
(908) 454-0700
www.sheridanprinting.com

Signature Book Printing, Inc.
8041 Cessna Ave. Ste. 132
Gaithersburg, MD 20879
(301) 258-8353
www.signature-book.com

Speedcolor, Inc. (POD)
4040 S.W. Adams St.
Peoria, IL 61605
(800) 373-2001
www.speedcolor.com

Sterling Pierce (POD)
422 Atlantic Ave.
East Rockaway, NY 11518
(516) 593-1170
www.sterlingpierce.com

Stinehour Press
853 Lancaster Rd.
Lunenburg, Vermont 05906
(800) 331-7753
www.stinehourpress.com

Sunshine Books
62 Decatur St.
Portsmouth, VA 23702
(757) 399-2577
www.sunshinebooks.prodigybiz.com

Technical Communication Services (POD)

110 West 12th Ave
North Kansas City, MO 64116
(816) 842-9770
www.tcsbook.com

Thomson-Shore, Inc.
7300 W. Joy Rd.
Dexter, Michigan 48130
(734) 426-3939
www.tshore.com

Today's Offset Impressions
21305 Forbes Rd.
Bedford, OH 44146
(440) 735-0850

Toppan Printing Co. of America
1100 Randolph Rd.
Somerset, NJ 08873
(732) 469-8400
www.ta.toppan.com

Total Printing Systems (POD)
103 E. Morgan
Newton, IL 62448
(800) 465-5200
www.tps1.com

Trade Printing Services, LLC
2080 Las Palmas Dr.
Carlsbad, CA 92009
(760) 496-0230 ext. 27
www.tradeprintingsvc.com

Trade Service Publications (POD)
10996 Torreyana Rd.
San Diego, CA 92121
(800) 854-1527
www.tradeservicepubs.com

Triart Graphics Inc.
234 Ridgedale Ave.
Cedar Knolls, NJ 07927

Tri-State Associated
Services (POD)
Tri-State Litho
71-81 Ten Broeck Ln
Kingston, NY 12401
(914) 331-1571
www.tristatelitho.com

UniMac Graphics
350 Michelle PL
Carlsadt, NJ
(201) 372-1000
www.unimacgraphics.com

United Book Press
1807 Whitehead Rd.
Baltimore, MD 21207
(410) 944-4044
(800) 726-0120

Van Volumes, Ltd.
2 Springfield St.
POB 314
Three Rivers, MA 01080
(413) 283-8556
(800) 290-0462

Vaughn Printing
411 Cowan St.
Nashville, TN 37207
(615) 256-2244
www.vaughnprinting.com

Webcom Limited
3480 Pharmacy Ave.
Toronto, Ontario M1W 2S7
(Canada)
(800) 665-9322
(416) 496-1000

West Coast Paradise
Publishing
Sardis Station
POB 2093
Sardis, BC V2R 1A5
(Canada)
(604) 824-9528
www.wcpar.com

Whitehall Printing Company
4244 Corporate Square
Naples, FL 34104
(800) 321-9290
www.whitehallprinting.com

WhitMar Electronic Press
(POD)
4885 Ronson Ct. Ste. E
San Diego, CA 92111
(858) 499-0050
www.whitmar.net

The Wimmer Companies
4650 Shelby Air Dr.
Memphis, TN 38118
(800) 548-2537
www.wimmerco.com

Offical Contact Pages: Resources

3. RESOURCES

American Bookseller
Association (ABA)
828 S. Broadway
Tarrytown, NY 10591
(800) 637-0037
www.BookWeb.org

Christian Booksellers
Association (CBA)
Trade association dedicated
to retail distribution of
Christian materials.
POB 62000
Colorado, Springs, CO
80962-2000
(800) 252-1950
www.cbaonline.org

National Association of
College Stores (NACS)
College Store Industry
Trade Aassociation.
500 E. Lorain St
Oberlin, OH 44074-1294
(800) 622-7498
www.nacs.org

The Book Trade in Canada
Directory that lists
everything from distributors
to government agencies.

70 The Esplanade Ste. 210
Toronto, Ontario M5E 1R2
(416) 360-0044
www.quillandquire.com/btic

National Library of Canada
Source for ISBN and CIP
info.
395 Wellington St.
Ottawa, Ontario K1A 0N4
(613 955-9481
www.nil-bnc.ca

4. ISBN & BARCODE SUPPLIERS

Aarongraphics
2903 Saturn St. Unit G
Brea, CA 92821
(714) 985-1290
(800) 345-8944
www.aarongraphics.com

Accession Inc.
6608 216th St. S.W. Ste. #105
Mountlake Terrace, WA 98043
(800) 531-6029
www.barcodes.org

Accugraphix
3588 E. Enterprise Dr.
Anaheim, CA 92807
(800) 872-9977
www.bar-code.com

Bar-Code Associates Inc.
3811 Mono Place
Santa Maria, CA 93455
(800) 876-1177
www.bar-code.cc

Barcode Graphics
1125 Eagle Park Rd.
Birmingham, AL 35242
(800) 662-0703
www.barcode-us.com

Bar Code Graphics Inc.
375 Fifth St.
Columbus, OH 43219
(800) 932-7801
www.barcode-graphics.com

Bar Code Label Systems
100 US Hwy 46
Mountain Lakes, NJ 07046
(800) 350-8234
www.BCLabel.com

Bar Codes Talk Inc.
7358 Broad St.
Brooksville, FL 34601
(352) 799-6070
(800) 728-4009
barcodes@tampabay.rr.com

E-Code Services
10401 E. Spry St.
Norwalk, CA 90650
(562) 864-6910
(877) 95-ECODE
ecodeservice@earthlink.net

Film Masters
11680 Hawke Rd.
Columbia Station, OH 44028
(800) 541-5102
www.filmmasters.com

Fotel Inc.
1125 E. Saint Charles RD. Ste. 100
Lombard, IL 60148
(630) 932-7520
(800) 834-4920
www.fotel.com

General Graphics
1608 Leishman Ave.
POB 3192
Arnold, PA 15068
(800) 887-5894
www.ggbarcode.com

Offical Contact Pages: ISBN & Barcode Suppliers

Infinity Graphics
2277 Science Pkwy.
Okemos, MI 48864
(800) 292-2633
www.infinitygraphics.com

Pacific Northwest Barcode
Services
POB 314
Medford, OR 97501
(800) 866-9721
www.pnwbooks.com

Paradox Systems Inc.
1187 N. Tustin Ave.
Anaheim, CA 92807
(800) 543-3319
Pdoxsys@aol.com

Product Identification &
Processing Systems Inc.
436 E. 87th St.
New York, NY 10128
(800) 358-7226
www.pips.com

R.R. Bowker LLC
630 Central Ave.
New Providence, NJ 07974
(800) 526-9537
www.bowker.com

Swing Labels, LLC
410 Great Rd. #B9
Littleton, MA 01460
(978) 486-3200
www.swinglabels.com

5. BOOK MANUFACTURERS

Acme Bookbinding
POB 290699
100 Cambridge St.
Charlestown, MA 02129
(800) 242-1821
(617) 242-1100
www.acmebook.com

Adams Press
6167 N. Broadway #236
Chicago, IL 60660
(312) 236-3838

Arvato Print USA
(Bertelsmann)
Dallas, PA
(570) 675-5261
www.ArvatoUSA.com

Bang Printing
1473 Hwy 18E
Brainerd, MN 56401-0587
(800-328-0450

Banta Corporation
225 Main St.
Menasha, WI 54952
(800) 291-1171

Bookmasters, Inc.
2541 Ashland RD.
Mansfield, OH 44905
(800) 537-6727

BRIOprint, LLC
1600 South Hwy 100 St 320
Minneapolis, MN 55416
(888) 333-7979
www.brioprint.com

Cadmus Communications
Richmond, VA
(804) 287-5680
www.cadmus.com

Central Plains Book Manufacturing
22234 "C" St.
Strother Field
Winifield, KS 67156
(877) 278-2726

CJK
Cincinnati, OH
(513) 271-6035
www.midlangcorp.com

CMYK Graphix Inc.
11322 N. Northtrail Dr.
Dunlap, IL 61525
(800) 698-2071
www.cmykgraphix.com

Commercial Communications Inc. (CCI)
Hartland, Wis
(262) 369-6000
www.comcom.com

Courier Corp.
N. Chelmsford, Mass
(978) 251-6000
www.courier.com

CMYK Graphix Inc.
11322 N. Northtrail Dr.
Dunlap, IL 61525
(800) 698-2071

Offical Contact Pages: Book Manufacturers

www.cmykgraphix.com

D.B. Hess, Inc.
1530 McConnell Rd.
Woodstock, Illinois 60098
(815) 338-6900

De HART's Printing Services
3333 Bowers Ave. Ste. 130
Santa Clara, CA 95054
(888) 982-4763

Diamond Publications
14061 Airport Blv.
Mobile, AL 36608
(251) 776-5717

Dickinson Press Inc.
Gtand Rapids, MI
(616) 957-5100
dickinsonpress.com

Documation
1556 International Dr.
Eau Claire, WI 54701
(800) 951-6729

Dorrance Publishing
701 Smithfield St. 3rd Fl
Pittsburgh, PA 15222

Edwards Brothers Inc.
2500 S. State St.
Ann Arbor, MI 48104
(734) 769-1000

Endeavor Printing
37-04 29th St.
Long Island City, NY 11101
(718) 570-2720
www.endeavorprinting.com

Friesens Corp.
Altona, Manitoba
(204) 324-6401

Hess Management Co.
Austin, TX
(512) 231-0900
www.hessmanagement.com

Hignall Book Printing
488 Burnell St.
Winnipeg, Manitoba R3G 2B4 (Canada)
(800) 304-5553

IBT Global
18 Industrial Park Rd.
Troy, NY 12180
(518) 271-5117

L.K. Litho
Middle Island, N.Y.
(631) 924-8555
www.linickgroup.com

Lake Book Manufacturing
2085 North Cornell Ave.
Melrose Park, IL 60160
(708) 345-7000

Lightning Source Inc.
1246 Heil Quaker Blv
La Vergne, TN 37086
(615) 213-5815
www.lightningsource.com

Malloy Inc.
5411 Jackson Rd.
Box 1124
Ann Arbor, MI 48106
(800) 722-3231

Apple-Vail Press Company
POB 2095
York, PA 17405
(717) 764-5911
www.Maple-Vail.com

Mazer Corporation
6680 Poe Ave.
Dayton, OH 45414
(937) 264-2600

McNaughton & Gunn
960 Woodland Dr.
Saline, MI 48176
(734) 429-5411

Midland Information Resources
Davenport, Iowa
(563) 359-3696
www.midlandcorp.com

Morgan Printing
900 Old Koenig Lane Ste. 135
Austin TX 78756
(512) 45-5194

NPC Inc.
Claysburg, PA
(814) 239-8787
www.npcweb.com
Network Printers, Inc.
1010 S. 70th St.
Milwaukee, WI 53214
(414) 443-0530

Offset Paperback Manufactures
Div. Bertelsman AG
POB N
Dallas, PA 18612

(570) 673-5261

The P.A. Hutchison Co.
Mayfield, PA
(570) 876-4560
www.pahutch.com

Pacific Rim International Printing
11924 Washington Blvd.
Las Angeles, CA 90066
(310) 390-3500

Phoenix Color Corp.
Hagerstown, MD
(301) 733-0018
www.phoenixcolor.com

Pneuma Books
327 Curtis Ave.
Elton, MD 21921
(410) 996-8900

The Press of Ohio
3765 Sunnybrook Rd.
Brimfield, OH 44240
(330) 678-5868

Print Local
7 Park Ave. Ste 24
New York, NY 10016
(877) 816-4448
www.printlocal.com

Printing Industry Exchange, LLC
POB 2238
Ashburn, VA 20146
(703) 631-4533
www.printindustry.com

Offical Contact Pages: Book Manufacturers

Publishers Express Press
Flambeau Litho Corp.
200 W. 5th St. S.POB 123
Ladysmith, WI 54848
(800) 255-9929
www.publishersexpresspress.com

QEP Design
4 Longfellow Rd.
Cambridge, MA 02138
(613) 499-1449

Quebecor World Inc.
Montreal
(514) 877-5317
www.quebecworld.com

R.R. Donelly
Chicago, IL
(800) 742-4455
www.rrdonnelley.com

Rose Printing Co. Inc.
Tallahassee, FL
(850) 576-4151
www.roseprinting.com

Sheridan Books
613 E. Industrial Dr.
Chelsea, MI 48118
(800) 999-2665

Solisco
Scott, Quebec
(418) 387-8908
www.solisco.com

Stromberg Allen and Company
3333 West 47th St
Chicago, IL 60632
(773) 847-7131

Transcontinental Inc.
Montreal
(514) 954-4000
www.transcontinental-GTC.com

Thomson-Shore
7300 W. Joy Rd.
Dexter, MI 48130
(734) 426-3939

United Graphics Inc.
1230 S. 57th Ave.
Cicero, Il 60804
(708) 780-7728
www.bookmanufacturing.com

Vail-Ballou Press
POB 1005
Binghamton, NY 13902
(607) 723-7981

Vaughn Printing
411 Cowan St.
Nashville, TN 37207
(615) 256-2244

Versa Press, Inc.
1465 Spring Bay Rd.
East Peoria, IL 61611
(800) 447-7829
www.versapress.com

Victor Graphic, Inc.
1211 Bernard Dr.
Baltimore, Maryland 21223
(410) 233-8300
www.victorgraphics.com

Visual Systems, Inc.
8111 N. 87th St.
Milwaukee, WI 53224
(414) 464-8333

Von Hoffman Corporate Offices
1000 Camera Ave.
St. Louis MO 63126
(314) 966-0909

Walsworth Publishing Company, Inc
306 N. Kansas Ave
Marceline, MO 64658
(800) 369-2646

Webcom
Toronto
(800) 665-9322
www.webcomlink.com

Webcrafters, Inc.
2211 Fordem Ave.
Madison, WI 53704
(608) 244-3561
www.webcrafters-inc.com

Westcan Printing Group
84 Durrand Rd.
Winnipeg, Manitoba R2J 3T2 (Canada)
(204) 669-9914

Whitehall Printing Company
4244 Corporate Square
Naples, FL 34104
(800) 321-9290

Worzalla Publishing Company
POB 307
Stevens Point, WI 54481
(715) 344-9600
www.worzalla.com

Offical Contact Pages: Book Distributors

6. BOOK DISTRIBUTORS

A Capella
Chicago Review Press
814 N. Franklin St.
Chicago, IL 60610
(312) 337-0747
fax: (312) 640-0342
www.ipgbook.com

A-R Editions Inc.
8851 Research Way Ste. 180
Middleton, WI 53562
(608) 836-9000
www.areditions.com

Abingdon Press
The United Methodist Publisheing House
201 Eigth Ave. S.
Nashville, TN 37203
(615) 749-6000
www.abingdon.org

Algora Publishing
222 Riverside Dr. 16th Fl
New York, NY 10025
(212) 678-0232
www.algora.com

All Wild-Up Productions
POB 1354
Puyallup, WA 98371
(206) 457-1949
www.allwildup.com

Acorn-Alliance Distribution Inc.
549 Old North Rd
Kingston, RI 02881
(800) 692-3786
www.moyerbellbooks.com

African Imprint Library Services
8122 Reynard Rd.
Chapel Hill, NC 27516
(919) 968-9417
www.africanbooks.com

Alliance Book Company
POB 7884
Hilton Head Island, SC 29938
(678) 361-3953

Alta Book Center
14 Adrian Ct.
Burlingame, CA 94010
(800) ALTA/ESL
www.altaesl.com

American International Distribution Corp. (AIDC)
50 Winter Sport Ln.
Williston, VT 05495
(800) 488-2665
www.aidcvt.com

American Multi-Cultural Publications
124 Reegar Ave.
Trenton NJ 08610
(609) 777-5533
www.diversity-books.com

Baker & Taylor Inc.
2550 W Tyvola Rd. Ste. 300
Charlotte, NC 28217
(800) 775-1800
www.btol.com

BCH Fulfillment &
Distribution
46 Purdy St.
Harrison, NY 10528
(800) 431-1579
www.bookch.com

Biblio Distribution
4501 Forbes Blvd. Ste. 200
Lanham, MD 20706
(800) 462-6420
www.bibliodistribution.com

Book Clearing House
46 Purdy St.
Harrison House, NY 10528
(800) 431-1579
www.bookch.com

BookMaster Inc.
30 Amberwood Pkwy.
Ashland, OH 44905
(800) 534-6727
www.bookmasters.com

Book Vine for Children
3980 Albany St.
McHenry, IL 60050
(815) 363-8880
www.bookvine.com

BookWorld Services Inc.
1933 Whitfield Park Look
Sarasota, FL 34243
(941) 758-8094
www.bookworld.com

Calvary Distribution
3232 MacArthur Blv. Ste. B
Santa Ana, CA 92704
(800) 444-7664
www.calvaryd.org

Canbook Distribution
Services
1220 Nicholson Rd.
New Market, Ontario L3Y
7V1(Canada)
(905) 836-5807
www.canbook.com

C & B Books Distribution
75-25 Parson's Blv.
Flushing, NY 11366
(718) 380-9555
www.cbbooksdistribution.com

Centax Books & Distribution
1150 Eighth Ave.
Regina SK S4R 1C9
(Canada)
(800) 823-6829
www.centaxbooks.com

Client Distribution Services
Inc.
425 Madison Ave.
New York, NY 10017
(800) 343-4499

Consortium Book Sales &
Distribution
1045 Westgate Dr. Ste. 90
St. Paul, MN 55114
(800) 283-3572
www.cbsd.com

Continental Books

Offical Contact Pages: Book Distributors

625 E. 70 Ave. Ste. 5
Denver, CO 80229
(800) 279-1764
www.continentalbook.com

CPG Distribution Inc.
POB 190694
Miami Beach, FL 33119
(305) 538-2495
cpgdistribution@juno.com

Disticor Direct Book Division
695 Westney Rd. S. Ste. 14
Ajax, ON L1S 6M9 (Canada)
(866) 679-2665
www.disticodirect.com

Empire Publishing Service
POB 1344
Studio City, CA 91614
(818) 784-8918

FaithWorks
9247 Hunterboro Dr.
Brentwood, TN 37027
(615) 221-6442
www.faithworksonline.com

GL Services
1957 Eastman Ave.
Ventura, CA 93003
(888) 610-8011
www.glservices.com

Greenleaf Book Group LLC
4425 Mopac South, Ste 600
Longhorn Bldg. 3rd FL
Austin, TX 78735
www.greenleafbookgroup.com

Independent Publishers Group

814 North Franklin St.
Chicago, IL 60610
(312) 337-0747
www.ipgbook.com

International Publishers Marketing
22841 Quicksilver Dr.
Sterling, VA 20166
(703) 661-1586
www.internationalpubmarket.com

Koen-Levy Book Wholesalers LLC
10 Twosome Dr. Box 600
Moorestown, NJ 08057
(800) 257-8481
www.koen.com

Lakeport Distributors Inc.
139 W. 18th St.
Erie, PA 16501
(814) 455-4461

Lightning Source Inc.
1246 Heil Quaker Blv.
La Vergne, TN 37086
(615) 213-5815
special.lightningsource.com/link.ingram.html

Metamorphous Press
POB 10616
Portland, OR 97296
(800) 937-7771
www.metamodels.com

Midpoint Trade Books Inc.
27 W. 20th St.
New York, NY 10011
(212) 727-0190
www.midpointtrade.com

Mint Publishing
62 June Rd.
New Salem, NY 10560
(914) 276-6576

National Book Network
4501 Forbes Blv. Ste. 200
Lanham, MD 20706
(301) 459-3366
www.nbnbooks.com

North Central Book Distributors
N57 W13636 Carmen Ave.
Menomonee Falls, WI 53051
(262) 781-3299
northcentralbook@sbcglobal.net

Owl Book Distributors Inc.
1021 Rte. 109
Farmingdale, NY 11735
(631) 249-9803

Partners Publishers Group
2325 Jarco Dr.
Holt, MI 48842
(517 694-320

Pathway Book Service
4 White Brook RD.
Gilsum, NH 03448
(800) 345-6665
pbs@pathwaybook.com

Printed Matter Inc.
535 W. 22nd St.
New York, NY 10011
(212) 925-0325
www.printedmatter.org

Prosperity & Profits Unlimited Distribution
POB 416
Denver, CO 80201
(303) 575-5676
www.prosperityandprofitsunlimited.com

Publishers Group West
1700 Fourth St.
Berkeley, California 94710
(800) 788-3123
www.pgw.com

Quality Books
1003 West Pines Rd.
Oregon, Illinois 61061
(800) 323-4241
www.quality-books.com

REM Distributors Inc.
POB 57
New Canaan, CT 06840
(203) 322-5352

Rights & Distribution Inc.
2131 Hollywood Blv. Ste. 305
Hollywood, FL 33020
(954) 925-5242

S & W Distributors Inc.
1600-H E Wendover Ave.
Greensboro, NC 27405
(336) 272-7394

SCB Distributors
15608 S. New Century Dr.
Gardena, CA 90248
(800) 729-6423
www.scbdistributors.com

SPD/ Small Press Distribution
1341 Seventh St.

Offical Contact Pages: Book Distributors

Berkeley, CA 94710
(800) 869-7553
www.spdbooks.org

Spring Arbor Contract
Distribution Services
One Ingram Blv.
La Vergne, TN 37086
(800) 395-4340
(800) 937-8100
www.springarbor.com

Tuttle Publishing
Airport Business Park
364 Innovation Dr.
N. Clarendon, VT 05759
www.tuttlepublishing.com

Victory Multimedia
460 Hindry Ave. Unit D
Inglewood, CA 90301
(310) 590-1388
www.victorymultimedia.com

Wilson & Associates
POB 2569
Alvin, TX 77511
(218) 388-0196
www.wilsonpublishing.com

A&B Books
223 Duffield Street
Brooklyn, NY 17201
877-542-6657

Seaburn Publishing
PO Box 2085
Long Island City, NY 11102
(718) 643-8202
info@seaburn.com

Lushena Books, Inc
607 Country Club Drive
Unit E
Bensenville, Il 60106
630-238-8824

7. PUBLISHERS

Allworth Press
10 E. 23rd St. Ste. 510
New York, NY 10010
Fax: (212) 777-8261
www.allworth.com

American Press
28 State St. Ste. 1100
Boston, MA 02109
(617) 247-0022

Arte Publico Press
University Of Houston
Houston, TX 77204
(713) 743-2841
www.arte.uh.edu

Aslan Publishing
2490 Black Rock Turnpike #342
Fairfield, CT 06432
(203) 372-0300
www.aslanpublishing.com

Avery
Penguin Putnam
375 Hudson St.
New York, NY 10014
www.penguinputnam.com

Barbour Publishing Inc.
POB 719
Uhrichsville, OH 44683
(740) 922-6045
www.barbourbooks.com

Barefoot Books
3 Bow St. 3rd Fl
Cambridge, MA 02138
(617) 576-0660
barefootbooks.com

Barricade Books Inc.
185 Bride Plaza N Ste . 308A
Fort Lee, NY 07024
(201) 944-7600

Basic Books
Perseus Books
10 E. 53rd St. 23rd Fl
New York, NY 11788
(631) 434-3311
www.barronseduc.com

BET Books
2000 M Street NW Suite 602
Washington, DC 20036
202 533-1970
www.betbooks.com

Beyond Works Publishing Inc.
20827 NW Cornell Rd. Ste. 500
Hillsboro, OR 97124
(503) 531-8700
www.beyondword.com

Black Classic Press
PO Box 1341
Baltimore, MD 21204
(410) 358-0980
(410 358-0987 fax

Black Dog & Leventhal Publishers
151 W. 19th St. 12 FL

Offical Contact Pages: Publishers

New York, NY 10011
(212) 647-9336

Black Pearl Books
3653-F Flakes Mill Road
PMB 306
Atlanta, Ga. 30034
404 735-3553

Bottom Dog Press
c/o Fireland College of BGSU
Huron, OH 44839
(419) 433-5560

Boyds Mills Press
Highlights of Children
815 Church St.
Honesdale, PA 18431
(570) 253-1164
www.boydsmillspress.com

Branden Publishing Co. Inc.
POB 812094
Wellesley, MA 02482
(781) 790-1056 fax
www.branden.com

Capital Books
22841 Quicksilver Dr.
Dulles, VA 20166
(703) 661-1533
www.capital-books.com

Coastal Carolina Press
2231 Wrightsville Ave.
Wilmington, NC 28403
www.coastalcarolinapress.org

Common Courage Press
One Red Barn Rd.
Box 702
Monroe ME 04951

(207) 525-0900
(800) 497-3207
www.commoncouragepress.com

Conquering books
210 Arrowhead Dr. Ste. #1
Charlotte, NC 28213
(704) 509-2226
www.conqueringbooks.com

Cricket Books
332 S. Michigan Ave. #1100
Chicago, IL 60604
(312) 939-1500
www.cricketbooks.net

Dafina Publishing
850 Third Avenue
New York, NY 10022
877-422-3665

May Davenport Publishers
26313 Purissima Rd.
Los Altos Hills, CA 94022
(650) 947-1275
www.maydavenportpublishers.com

Descant Publishing
POB 12973
Mill Creek, WA 98082
(206) 235-3357
www.descantpub.com

The Design Image Group Inc.
231 Frontage RD. Ste 17
Burr Ridge, IL 60521
(630) 789-8991
www.designimagegroup.com

Diogenes Publishing
965 Alamo Dr. Unit 336

Vacaville, CA 95687
(707) 447-6482
www.diogenespublishing.com

Dover Publications Inc.
31 E. 2nd St.
Mineola, NY 11501
(516) 294-7000
www.publications.com

Dufour Editions
POB 7
Chester Springs, PA 19425
(610) 458-5005
www.dufoureditions.com

Eastland Press
POB 99749
Seattle, WA 98199
(206) 217-0204
www.eastlandpress.com

Electric Works Publishing
605 Ave. C.E.
Bismarck, ND 58501
(701) 255-0356
www.electricpublishing.com

Executive Excellence Publishing
1366 E. 2210 S.
Provo, UT 84606
(800) 304-9782
www.eep.com

Fairview Press
2450 Riverside Ave.
Minneapolis, MN 55454
(800) 544-8207
www.fairviewpress.org

Focus Publishing Inc.
POB 665
Bemidji, MN 56619
(218) 759-9817

Front Street
20 Batter Park Ave. #403
Asheville, NC 28801
(828) 236-3097
www.frontstreetbooks.com

Future Horizons
721 W. Abram St.
Arlington, TX 76013
(817) 277-0727
www.futurehorizons-autism.com

Green Park Press
POB 1108
Bridgeport, CT 06601
(203) 372-4861
www.greenbarkpress.com

Grove/Atlantic, Inc.
841 Broadway
New York, NY 10003
212 614-7850
212 614-7886

Gospel Light Publications
2300 Knoll Drive
Ventura, Ca 93003
805-644-9721

G Unit Books
1230 Avenue Of the Americas
New York, NY 10020
212 868-7000
800 223-2336
www.simonsays.com

Offical Contact Pages: Publishers

Guild Press, Emmis Publishing LP
10665 Andrade Dr.
Zionsville, IN 46077
(317) 733-4175
www.guildpress.com

Hampton Roads Publishing Company Inc.
1125 Stoney Ridge RD.
Charlottesville, VA 22902
(434) 296-2772
hrpub.com

Harlequin Books/
Silhouette Books
233 Broadway, Suite 1001
New York, NY 10279
212 553-4200

Harcourt Children's Books
15 East 26th Street
New York, NY 10010
212 592-1000

Hawk Publishing Group
71075 Yale Ave. #345
Tulsa, OK 74136
www.hawkpub.com

The Haworth Press Inc.
10 Alice St.
Binghamton, NY 13904
(607) 722-5857
www.haworthpressinc.com

Hazelden Publishing and Educational Services
15251 Pleasant Valley Rd.
Center City, MN 55012
(651) 257-4010
www.hazelden.org

Heridias
185 Bridge Plaza Ste. 308-A
Fort Lee, NJ 07024
(201) 944-7600
www.herodias.com

Hill Street Press, LLC
191 E Broad Street, suite 209
Athens, Ga 30601-2848
706 613-7200
706 613-7204

Hill and Wang
Farrar Straus & Giroux Inc.
19 Union Square W.
New York, NY 10003
(212) 741-6900

Houghton Mifflin Company
215 Park Ave South
New York, NY 10003
212 420-5800
www.hmco.com

Howells House
POB 9546
Washington DC 20016
(202) 333-2182

Imajinn Books
POB 162
Hickory Corners, MI 49060
(616) 671-4633
www.imajinnbooks.com

Infinite Possibilities Publishing Group Inc.
POB 150823
Altamonte, Springs, FL 32715
(407) 699-6603
www.IPpublishingOnline.com

Interlink Publishing Group Inc.
46 Crosby St.
Northampton, MA 01060
(413) 582-7054
www.interlinkbooks.com

Jameson Books Inc.
722 Columbus St.
Ottawa, IL 61350
(815) 434-7905
(815) 434-7907

JustWRITE Publishing
POB V-46
Palo Alto, CA 94304
1 866 337-3201
www.justwritepublishing.com

Kensington Publishing Corp.
850 Third Ave. 16th FL
New York, NY 10022
(212) 407-1500
www.kensingtonbooks.com

Koenisha Publications
3196 53rd St.
Hamilton, MI 49419
(616) 751-4100
www.koenisha.com

LadyBugPress
751 Laurel St. #223
San Carlos, CA 94070
www.ladybugpress.com

Langmarc Publishing
POB 90488
Austin, TX 78709
(512) 394-0989
www.langmarc.com

Loft Press Inc
POB 126
Fort Valley, VA 22652
(540) 933-6210
www.loftpress.com

Love Spell
Dorchester Publishing Co. Inc
276 Fifth Ave. Ste. 1008
New York, NY 10001
www.dorchesterpub.com

The Lyons Press
246 Goose Lane
Gillford, CT 06437
(203) 458-4500
www.lyonspress.com

Macadam/Cage PublishingInc
155 Sansome St. Ste. 620
San Francisco, CA 94104
(415) 986-7502
www.macadamcage.com

Meriweather Publishing LTD.
885 Elkton Dr.
Colorado Springs, CO 80907
(719) 594-4422
merpeds@aol.com

Milkweeds for Young Readers
1011 Washington Ave. S. Ste. 300
Minneapolis, MN 55415
(612) 332-3192
www.milkweed.org

Mind's Eye Publishing
POB 38114
St. Louis, MO 63138
(314) 495-0220

Offical Contact Pages: Publishers

mymindseye.net

Moody Press
820 North Lasalle Blvd.
Chicago, Il 60610-3284
312-329-2101
800-678-8812
www.moodypress.org

Narwhal Press Inc.
1629 Meeting St.
Charleston, SC 29405
(843) 853-0510
www.shipwrecks.com

New American Library
375 Hudson St.
New York, NY 10014
(212) 366-200
www.penguinputnam.com

New Century Books
Sharon's Books
POB 7113
The Woodlands, TX 77387
(936) 295-5357

The New England Press Inc.
POB 575
Shelburne, VT 05482
(802) 863-2520
www.nepress.com

New Victoria Publishers
POB 27
Norwich VT 05055
(802) 649-5297
www.opendoor.com/NewVic/

New Voices Publishing
POB 560 Wilimington, MA
01887

(978) 658-2131
www.kidsterrain.com

NW Writer's Corporation
30620 Pacific Hwy S. Ste. 110
Federal Way, WA 98003
(253) 839-3177
www.nwwriterscorp.com

Oak Tree Press
915 Foothill Blv #411
Claremont, CA 91711
(909) 625-8400
www.oaktreebooks.com

The Oaklea Press
6912-B Three Chopt Rd.
Richmond, VA 23226
(804) 281-5872
www,oakleapress.com

Odd Girls Press
POB 2157
Anaheim, CA 92814
(800) 821-0632
www.oddgirlspress.com

One World Books
1540 Broadway 11th Fl
New York, NY 10036
(212) 782-8378
adiggs@randomhouse.com

Open Hand Publishing LLC
Greensboro, NC
(336) 292-8585
www.openhand.com

Orchard Books
557 Broadway

New York, NY 10012
(212) 343-6100

Richard C. Owens Publishers Inc.
POB 585
Katonah, NY 10536
(914) 232-3903
www.rcowen.com

Peachtree Children's Books
1700 Chattahoochee Ave.
Atlanta, GA 30318
(404) 876-8761
www.peachtree-online.com

Peachtree Publishers LTD
1700 Chattahoochee Ave.
Atlanta, GA 30318
(404) 876-8761
www.peachtree-online.com

Pineapple Press, Inc.
POB 3889
Sarasota, FL 34230
(941) 359-0886

Pippin Press
229 E. 85th St.
POB 1347
Gracie Station
New York, NY 10028
(212) 288-4920
(732) 225-1562 fax

Plexus Publishing Inc.
143 Old Marlton Pike
Medford, NJ 08055
(609) 654-6500
jbryans@infotoday.com

Polychrome Publishing Corporation
4509 N. Francisco
Chicago, IL 60625
(773) 478-4455
www.polychromebooks.com

Regan Books
10 E. 53rd St.
New York, NY 10022
(212) 207-7400
www.harpercollins.com

Renaissance House
9400 Lloydcrest Dr.
Beverly Hills, CA 90210
(310) 358-5288
www.renaissancehouse.net

Resource Publications Inc.
160 E. Virginia St. Ste. 290
San Jose, CA 98112
(408) 286-8505
www.rpinet.com/ml

Rising Moon
POB 1389
Flagstaff, AZ 86002
(928) 774-5251
www.northlandpub.com

Rising Tide Press
POB 30457
Tucson, AZ 85751
(520) 888-1140
www.risingtidepress.com

River City Publishing
610 N. Perry St.
Montgomery, AL 36104
(334) 265-6753

Offical Contact Pages: Publishers

rivercitypublishing.com

RJ Publications
842 South 18th St. Suite 3
Newark, NJ 07108
973-373-2445

Roc Books
375 Hudson St.
New York, NY 10014
(212) 366-2000
www.penguinputnam.com

Royal Fireworks Publishing
1 First Ave.
POB 399
Unionville, NY 10988
(845) 726-4444
www.rfpress.com

Rutgers University Press
100 Joyce Kilmer Ave.
Piscataway, NJ 08854
(732) 445-7762
rutgerspress.rutgers.edu

Sandcastle Publishing
POB 3070
South Pasadena, CA 91030
(800) 891-4204
www.sandcastle-online.com

Sankofa World Publishers
POB 473592
Brooklyn, New York 11247
www.sankofaworldpublishers.com

Sarabande Books Inc.
2234 Dundee Rd. Ste. 200
Louisville, KY 40205
(502) 458-4028
www.sarabendebooks.org

Science & Humanities Press
POB 7151
Chesterfield, MO 63006
(636) 394-4950
www.sciencehumanitiespress.com

Scrivenery Press
POB 740969
Houston, TX 77274
(713) 665-6760
www.scrivenery.com

Silver Dagger Mysteries
The Overmountain Press
POB 1261
Johnson City, TN 37605
(423) 926-2691
www.silverdaggermysteries.com

Smart Cookie Publishing
2017 W. 15th Ave
Vancouver BC V6J 2L4
(Canada)
(604) 228-1711
www.webpotter.com/smartcookie

Soft Skull Press Inc.
107 Norfolk St.
New York, NY 10002
(212) 673-2502
www.softskull.com

Soho Press Inc.
853 Broadway
New York, NY 10003
(212) 260-1900
www.sohopress.com

Spinsters Ink
POB 2205

Denver, CO 80222
(303) 761-5552
www.spinsters-ink.com

Strebor Books International
PO Box 6505
Largo, MD 20792
301-583-0616
800-223-2336

Stonewall Inn
St. Martin's Press
175 Fifth Ave.
New York, NY 10010
(212) 674-5151
www.stonewallinn.com

Teri Woods Publishing
Greeley Square Station
PO Box 20069
New York, NY 10001-005
212 252-8445
212 252-8494
www.teriwoodspublishing.com

Third World Press
POB 19730
Chicago, IL 60619
(773) 651-0700
TWpress3@aol.com

Megan Tingley Books
Little Brown & Co.
Three Center Plaza
Boston, MA 02108
(617) 227-0730
www.twbookmark.com

Triple Crown Publications
4449 Easton Way 2nd Fl.
Columbus, Ohio 43219
614-934-1233

Turtle Books
866 United Nations Plaza
Ste. 525
New York, NY 10017
(212) 644-2020
www.turtlebooks.com

Underground Epics
Publishing Inc.
Atlanta, GA 30310
(800) 757-0539
www.undergroundepics.com

Upstart Books
POB 800
Fort Atkinson, WI 53538
(920) 563-9571
www.highsmith.com

Vista Publishing Inc.
422 Morris Ave. Ste. #1
Long Beach, NJ 07740
(732) 229-6500
www.vistapubl.com

Voices of Truth Publishing
POB 34
Donalds, South Carolina
29638
(864) 379-8651
www.voiceoftruths.com

Waltsan Publishing LLC
5000 Barnett St.
Fort Worth, TX 76103
(817) 654-2978
www.waltsan.com

White Mane Books
63 W. Burd St.
POB 152
Shippensburg, PA 17257

Offical Contact Pages: Publishers

(717) 532-2237
www.whitemane.com

Albert Whitman and Co.
6340 Oakton St.
Morton Grove, IL 60053
(847) 581-0033
www.awhitmanco.com

Willowgate Press
POB 6529
Holliston, MA 01746
(508) 429-8774
www.willowgatepress.com

WW Norton & Company, inc
500 Fifth Avenue
New York, NY 10110
212 354-5500
212 869-0856 fax
www.wwnorton.com

Zondervan Publishing House
5300 Patterson Ave Se
Grand Rapids, MI 49530
616-698-6900
616-698-3454 fax
www.zondervan.com

Life Changing Books
P.O. Box 421
Brandywine, MO 20613
www.lifechanging.net

Q-Boro Books
165-41A Baisley Blvd.
Jamaica, New York 11434
www.QBorobooks.com

Car San Publishing
2439 Sunridge Avenue
Atlanta, Ga. 30315
404 627-3427
404 627-8132 fax
cssperry@yahoo.com

Publishing Associates, Inc.
5020 Montcalm Drive
Atlanta, Ga. 30331-8421
fcpublish@aol.com

Kimani Press
233 Broadway
New york, NY 10279
www.kimanipress.com

Augustus Publishing
33 indian Road Suite 3K
New York, 10034
www.augustuspublishing.com

Urban Books
10 Brennan Place
Deer park, NY 11726
www.urbanbooks.net

BET Books
2000 M Street NW Suite 602
Washington, DC 20036

Urban Lifestyle Press
PO Box 12714
Charlotte, NC 28220

8. LITERARY AGENTS

Abraham House International
POB 200951
Arlington, TX 76006
(817) 794-0911
www.abrahamhouseintl.com

Alive Communications Inc.
7680 Goddard St. Ste 200
Colorado Springs, CO 80920
(719) 260-7080
www.alivecom.com

Altair Literary Agency LLC
POB 11656
Washington DC 20008
(202) 237-8282
www.altairliteraryagency.com

Appleseeds Management
200 E. 30th St. Ste. 302
San Bernardino, CA 92404
(909) 882-1667

Arcadia
31 Lake Place North
Danbury, CT 06810
arcardialit@att.net

Artists and Artisans Inc.
104 West 29th St. 11 Fl
New York, NY 10001
(212) 924-9619
www.artistsandartisans.com

Authentic Creations Literary Agency
875 Lawerenceville-Suwanee Rd. Ste. 310-306
Lawerenceville, GA 30043
(770) 339-3774
www.authenticcreations.com

Authors & Artists Group Inc.
41 E. 11th St. 11th Fl
New York, NY 10003
(212) 944-9898

The Author's Clearinghouse
7319 Locklin St.
West Bloomfield, MI 48324
(248) 363-5490
www.literaryclearinghouse.com

Balkin Agency Inc.
POB 222
Amherst, MA 01004
(413) 548-9835

Loretta Barrett Books Inc.
101 Fith Ave.
New York, NY 10003
(212) 807-9579
www.lorettabarretbooks.com

Meredith Bernstein Literary Agency
2112 Broadway Ste. 503A
New York, NY 10023
(212) 799-1007

Big Score Preoductions Inc.
POB 4575
Lancaster, PA 17604
(717) 293-0247
www.bigscoreproductions.com

Offical Contact Pages: Literary Agents

Bleecker Street Associates Inc.
532 LaGuardia Pl. # 617
New York, NY 10012
(212) 677-4492

Book Deals, Inc.
244 Fifth Ave, Suite 2164
New York, NY 10001-7604
212 252-2701
212 591-6211

Bookends LLC
136 Long Hill RD.
Gillette, NJ 07933
(908) 362-0090
www.bookends-inc.com

George Borchardt, inc
136 E. 57th Street
New York, NY 10022
212 753-5785
212 838-6518

Joan Brandt Agency
788 Wesley Dr.
Atlanta, GA 30305
(404) 351-8877

Andrea Brown Literary Agency Inc.
1076 Eagle Dr.
Salinas, CA 93905
(831) 422-5925
ablit@redshift.com

Curtis Brown, LTD
10 Astor Place
New York, NY 10003
212 473-5400

Sheree Bykofsky Associates Inc.
577 2nd ave. PMB 109
New York, NY 10016
www.shreebee.com

Carlisle & Co.
6 W. 18th St.
New York, NY 10011
(212) 813-1881
www.carlisleco.com

Castiglia Literary Agency
1155 Camino Del Mar Ste. 510
Del Mar, CA 92014
(858) 755-8761

Ruth Cohen Inc. Literary Agency
POB 2244
La Jolla, CA 92038
(858) 456-5805

The Cooke Agency
278 Bloor St. E. Ste. 305
Toronto, ON M4W 3M4 (Canada)
(416) 406-3390
agents@cookeagency.ca

Cornerstone Literary Inc.
4500 Wilshire Blv. 3rd Fl
Los Angeles, CA 90010
(323) 930-6039
www.cornerstoneliterary.com

Crawford Literary Agency
94 Evans Rd.
Barnstead, NH 03218
(603) 269-5851
crawfordlit@att.net

Richard Curtis Associates, inc
171 East 74th Street
New York, NY 10021
212 772-7363
212 772-7393 fax

The Cypher Agency
816 Wolcott Ave.
Beacon, NY 12508
(845) 831-5677
jimcypher@prodigy.net

David Black Literary Agency
156 Fifth Avenue
New York, NY 10010
212 242-5080
212 924-6609

Defiore & Co.
72 Spring St. Ste. 304
New York, NY 10012
(212) 925-7744
www.defioreandco.com

Susan Donahue
Harris, Harris & Donahue Ltd.
POB 4345
Wheaton, IL 60189
harris-donahue.tripod.com

Doyen Literary Services Inc.
1931 660th St.
Newell IA 50568
(712) 272-3300
www.barbaradoyen.com

Dunham Literary Inc.
156 Fifth Ave. Ste. 625
New York, NY 10010
(212) 929-0994
www.dunhamlit.com

Dupree/ Miller and Associates Inc. Literary
100 Highland Park Village Ste. 350
Dallas, TX 78205
(214) 559-BOOK
dmabook@aol.com

Dystel & Goderich Literary Management
1 Union Square W. Ste. 904
New York, NY 10003
(212) 627-9100
www.dystel.com

Easley Literary Agency LLC
POB 42119
Atlanta, GA 30311
www.easleylit.netfirms.com

Ethan Ellenberg Literary Agency
548 Broadway #5-E
New York, NY 10012
(212) 941-4652
www.ethanellenberg.com

Nicholas Ellison
55 Fifth Ave. 15th Fl
New York, NY 10003
(212) 206-6050
www.greenburger.com

Elaine P. English
Graybill & English LLC
1875 Connecticut Ave. Ste. 712
Washington DC 20009
(202) 588-9798 ext. 143
www.graybillandenglish.com

Offical Contact Pages: Literary Agents

Felicia Eth Literary Representation
555 Bryant St. Ste. 350
Palo Alto CA
(650) 401-8892
feliciaeth@aol.com

Farber Literary Agency Inc.
14 E. 75th St. #2E
New York, NY 10021
(212) 861-7075
www.donaldfarber.com

B.R. Fluery Agency
POB 149352
Orlando, FL 32814
(407) 895-8494
(888) 310-8142
brfleuryagency@juno.com

Folio Literary Management
240 W. 35th St. Ste. 500
New York, NY 10001
www.foliolit.com

Foster Literary Agency
9173 S. Vista West Dr.
West Jordan, UT 84088
fosterliterary@yahoo.com

The Gislason Agency
219 Main St. SE Ste. 506
Minneapolis, MN 55414
(612) 331-8033
www.gislasonagency.com

Goldfarb & Associates
721 Gibbon St.
Alexandria, VA 22314
(202) 466-3030
rglawlit@aol.com

Frances Goldin Literary Agency
57 E. 11th St. Ste. 5B
New York, NY 10003
(212) 777-0047
www.goldinlit.com

Goldleaf Publishing
330 IL Hwy 141
Norris City, IL 62869
www.goldleafpublishing.com

Sanford J. Greenburger Associates Inc.
55 Fifth Ave.
New York, NY 10003
(212) 206-5600
www.greenburger.com

Jill Grosjean Literary Agency
1390 Millstone Rd.
Sag Harbor NY 11963
(631) 725-7419
www.hometown.aol.com/jill6981/myhomepage/index.html

J Haggard Literary Agency
3825 SE 32nd #2
Portland, OR 97202
www.jhaggardliteraryagency.com

Reece Halsey
98 Main St.
Tiburon, CA 94920
(310) 62-7595 fax
www.reecehalseynorth.com

The Joy Harris Literary Agency inc.
156 Fifth ave. Ste. 617
New York, NY 10010

———————— *James Hickman* ————————

(212) 924-6269
gen.office@jhlitagent.com

Hartline Literary Agency
123 Queenston.dr.
Pittsburg, PA 15235
(412) 829-2495
www.hartlineliterary.com

Richard Henshaw Group
127 W. 24th St. 4th Fl
New York, NY 10011
(212) 414-1172
www.rich.henshaw.com

Jeff Herman Agency LLC
POB 1522
Stockbridge, MA 01262
(413) 298-0077
www.jeffherman.com

Hornfischer Literary
Management Inc.
POB 50544
Austin, TX 78763
www.hornfischerliterarymanagement.com

Intellectual Property
Management Group (IPMG)
Fax: (302) 371-5362
www.ipmg.net

Jabberwocky Literary
Agency
POB 4558
Sunnyside, NY 11104
(718) 392-5985

Natasha Kern Literary
Agency
POB 2908
Portland, OR 97208

(503) 297-6190
www.natashakern.com

Virginia Kidd Agency, inc
538 E. Hartfoed Street
PO Box 278
Milford, Pa 18337-0278
570 296-6205
570 296-7266 fax

Kissed Publications
POB 9819
Hampton , VA 23670
(757) 722-3031
www.kissedpublications.com

Harvey Klinger Inc.
301 W. 53rd St. Ste. 21-A
New York, NY 10019
(212) 581-7068
www.harveyklinger.com

The Knight Agency
577 S. Main St.
Madison, GA 30650
www.knightagency.net

Eddie Kritzer Productions
8484 Wilshire Blvd. Ste. 205
Beverly Hills, CA 90211
(323) 655-5696
www.eddiekritzer.com

Langtons International
Agency
240 West 35th St Ste. 500
New York, NY 10001
Langtonsinternational.com
Paul S. Levine Literary
Agency
1054 Superba Ave.

Offical Contact Pages: Literary Agents

Venice, CA 90291
(310) 450-6711
www.netcom.com

Robert Lieberman Associates
400 Nelson Rd.
Ithaca, NY 14850
(607) 273-8801
www.people.cornell.edu/pages/rhl10

Lindsey's Literary Services
7502 Greenville Ave. Ste. 500
Dallas, TX 75231
(214) 890-4050
bonedges001@aol.com

The Literary Group
270 Lafayette St. 1505
New York, NY 10012
(212) 274-1616
www.theliterarygroup.com

Carol Mann Agency
55 Fifth Avenue
New York, NY 10003
212 206-5635
212 675-4809

Manus & Associates Literary Agency Inc.
425 Sherman Ave. Ste. 200
Palo Alto, CA 94306
(650) 470-5151
www.manuslit.com

March Tenth Inc.
4 Myrtle St.
Haworth, NJ 07641
(201) 387-6551
www.marchtenthinc.com

Martin Literary Management
17328 Ventura Blvd. Ste. 138
Encino, CA 91316
(818) 595-1130
www.martinliterarymanagement.com

Donald Maas Literary Agency
160 W. 95th Street Suite 1B
New York, NY 10025
212 866-8200

McHugh Literary Agency
1033 Lyon RD.
Moscow, ID 83843
(208) 882-0107
elisabetmch@turbonet.com

William Morris Agency Inc.
1325 Avenue of the Americas
New York, NY 10019
(212) 586-5100
www.wma.com

Dee Maura Literary
269 West Shore Dr.
Massapequa, NY 11758
(516) 795-8797
samurai5@ix.netcom.com

National Writers Literary Agency
3140 S. Peoria #295
Aurora, CA 80014
(720) 851-1959
aajwiii@aol.com

The Novel Idea

9351 Westside Rd.
Anthony, NM 88021
(505) 882-7308
www.thenovelidea.com

Kathi J. Paton Literary
Agency
19 W. 55th St.
New York, NY 10019
(908) 647-2117
KJPLitBiz@aol.com

L. Perkins Associates
16 W. 36 Street
New York, NY 10018
212 279-6418
718 943-5354 fax

PHH Literary Agency
POB 724558
Atlanta, GA 31139
(678) 485-8871
www.phhliteraryagency.com

Alison Picard, Literary Agent
POB 2000
Cotuit, MA 02635
(508) 477-7192
ajpicard@aol.com

Alicka Pistek Literary
Agency LLC
302A W. 12th St. #124
New York, NY 10014
www.alickapistek.com

Julie Popkin
15340 Albright St. #204
Pacific Palisades, CA 90272
(310) 459-2834

QCorp Literary & Screen
Agency
POB 8
Hillsboro, OR 97123
(503) 680-6049
www.qcorplit.com

Quicksilver Books Literary
Agents
508 Central Park Ave.
#5101
Scarsdale, NY 10583
(914) 722-4664
www.quicksilverbooks.com

Regal Literary Agency
52 Warfield St.
Montclair, NJ 07043
(973) 509-5767
www.regal-literary.com

Resource/Arts
25 Highland Park Village
Ste. 100
Dallas, TX 75205
(254) 399-9784
(214) 324-8008

Jody Rhodes Literary
Agency
8840 Villa La Jolla Dr. Ste. 315
La Jolla, CA 92037
(858) 625-0544

Barbara Rifkind Literary
Agency
132 Perry St. 6th Fl
New York, NY 10014
(212) 229-0453
Barbara@barbararikind.net

Offical Contact Pages: Literary Agents

Ann Rittenberg Literary Agency Inc.
1201 Broadway Ste. 708
New York, NY 10001
(212) 684-6936

Riverside Literary Agency
41 Simon Keets Rd.
Leyden, MA 01337
(413) 772-0067
rivlit@sover.net

RLR Associaites LTD
Literary Dept.
7 W. 51st St.
New York, NY 10019
(212) 541-8641
www.rlrliterary.net

B.J. Robbins Literary Agency
5130 Bellaire Ave.
North Hollywood CA 91607
(818) 760-6602
robbinsliterary@aol.com

Linda Roghaar Literary Agency Inc.
133 High Point Dr.
Amherst, MA 01002
(413) 256-2636
www.lindaroghaar.com

Rosenberg Group
23 Lincoln Ave.
Marblehead, MA 01945
(781) 990-1341
www.rosenberggroup.com

The Gail Ross Literary Agency
1666 Connecticut Ave. NW #500
Washington DC 20009
(202) 328-3282
www.gailross.com

Victoria Sanders & Associates
241 Ave of the Americas
New York, NY 10014
(212) 633-8811
www.victoriasanders.com

Sedgeband Literary Associates
7312 Martha Ln.
Fort Worth, TX 76112
(817) 496 -3652
www.sedgeband.com

Serendipity Literary Agency LLC
732 Fulton St. Ste. 3
Brooklyn, NY 11238
(718) 230-7829
www.serendipitylit.com

Wendy Sherman Associates Inc.
450 Seventh Ave. Ste. 3004
New York, NY 10123
(212) 279-8863
wendy@wsherman.com

Irene Skolnick Literary Agency
22 W. 23rd St. 5th FL
New York, NY 10010
(212) 727-1024
sirene35@aol.com

Beverley Slopen Literary Agency
131 Bloor St. Ste. 711

Toronto, ON M5S 1S3
(Canada)
(416) 964-9598
www.slopenagency.com

Michael Snell Literary
Agency
POB 1206
Truro, MA 02666
(508) 349-3718

Southern Literary Group
Div. L. Perkins Associates
43 Stamford Dr.
Lakeview AR 72642
(870) 431-7006
southernlitgroup@yahoo.com

Stylus Literary Agency
275 Madison Ave. 4Th Fl
New York, NY 10016
www.stylusagency.com

Thoth Literary Agency
POB 620277
Littleton, CO 80162
(720) 351-9551
www.hawaiianhulahips.com/
thothliteraryagency

Three Seas Literary Agency
POB 7038
Madison, WI 53708
(608) 221-4306
www.threeseaslit.com

Ann Tobias Literary Agency
for Children's Books
520 E. 84th St. Apt. 4L
New York, NY 10028

Linda Tolls Literary Agency

POB 1785
Bend, OR 97709
(541) 388-3510
blswarts@juno.com

Venture Literary
8895 Towne Centre Dr. Ste.
105 #141
San Diego, CA 92122
(619) 807-1887
www.ventrueliterary.com

The Vines Agency
648 Broadway Ste. 901
New York, NY 10012
(212) 777-5522
www.vinesagency.com

John A. Ware Literary
Agency
392 Central Park West
New York, NY 10025
(212) 866-4733

Waterside Productions Inc.
2187 Newcastle Ave. #204
Cardiff-by-the-Sea, CA
92007
(760) 632-9190
www.waterside.com

Waxman Literary Agency
Inc.
1650 Broadway Ste. 1011
New York, NY 10019
www.waxmanagency.com

Wecksler-Incomco
170 West End Ave.
New York, NY 10023
(212) 787-2239

Offical Contact Pages: Literary Agents

Ted Weinstein Literary
Management
287 Duncan St. Dept. G
San Francisco, CA 94131
www.twliterary.com

Weiser & Elwell Inc.
80 Fifth Ave. Ste. 1101
New York, NY 10011
(212) 260-0860

Writers House
21 W. 26th St.
New York, NY 10010
(212) 685-2400

Bullet Entertainment Group
5441 riverdale Rd#129
College Park, GA 30349
404-246-6496
www.bentpublishing.com

9. SUGGESTED RESOURCES

Self-Publishing Resources
All-By-Yourself Self-Publishing
By David H. Li (Premier Pub Company)
PO Box 341267, Bethesda, MD 20827
e-mail: davidli@erols.com

The Art of Self-Publishing
By Bonnie Stahlman Speer (Reliance Press)
60-64 Hardinge Street, Denilquin, NSW, 2710; Australia
e-mail: reliance@reliancepress.com.au

Book Production: Composition, Layout, Editing, & Design.
Getting It Ready for Printing
By Dan Poynter (Para Publishing)
PO Box 8206-240, Santa Barbara, CA 93118-8206
805-968-7277; fax 805-968-1379; cellular: 805-680-2298
email: DanPoynter@aol.com,
75031.3534@compuserve.com

Business and Legal Forms for Authors and Self-Publishers
By Tad Crawford)Allworth Press)
10 East 23rd Street, Suite 210, New York, NY 10010
212-777-8395

The Complete Guide to Self-Publishing: Everything You Need to Know
to Write, Publish, Promote and Sell Yur Own Book
By Tom Ross, Marilyn J. Ross (Writers Digest Books)
1507 Dana Avenue, Cincinnati, OH 45207
513-531-222; fax: 513-531-4744

The Complete Guide to Successful Publishing
by Avery Cardoza (Cardoza Pub)
132 Hastings Street, Brooklyn, NY 11235
800-577-WINS, 718-743-5229; fax: 718-743-8284

Offical Contact Pages: Suggested Resources

e-mail: cardozapub@aol.com

The Complete Self-Publishing Handbook
By David M. Brownstone, Irene M. Franck (Plume)
375 Hudson Street, New York, NY 10014
212-366-2000

The Economical Guide to Self-Publishing: How to Produce and Market Your Book on a Budget
By Linda Foster Radke, Mary E. Hawkins , Editor (Five Star Publications)
PO Box 6698, Chandler, AZ 85246-6698
480-940-8182

Experts/Foreign Rights, Selling U.S. Books Abroad
By Dan Poynter (Para Publishing)
PO Box 8206-240, Santa Barbara, CA 93118-8206
805-968-7277; fax: 805-968-1379; cellular: 805-680-2298
e-mail: DanPoynter@aol.com,
75031.3534@compuserve.com

A Guide to Successful Self-Publishing
By Stephen Wagner (Prentice Hall Direct)
240 Frisch Court, Paramus, NJ 07652
201-909-6200

How to Make Money Publishing from Home, Revised 2nd Edition:
Everything You Need to Know to Successfully Publish Books, Newsletters,
Web Sites, Greeting Cards, and Software
By Lisa Shaw (Prima Publishing)
3000 Lava Ridge Court, Roseville, CA 95661

How to Publish Your Own Book and Earn $50,000 Profit
by Gordon Burgett (Communication Unlimited)
PO Box 6405, Santa Maria, CA 93456
800-563-1454; fax: 805-937-3035; e-mail:
Gordon@sops.com

How to Publish, Promote, and Sell Your Own Book

by Robert Lawrence Holt (St. Martin's Press)
175 Fifth Avenue, New York, NY 10010
212-674-5151

How to Self-Publish & Market Your Own Book: A Simple Guide for Aspiring Writers
by Mark E. Smith, Sara Freeman Smith (U R Gems Group)
POB 440341, Huoston, TX 77244-0341
281-596-8330

How to Self-Publish Your Book with Little or No Money! A Complete Guide to Self-Publishing at a Profit!
By Bettie E. Tucker, Wayne Brumagin
(Rainbow's End Company)
354 Golden Grove Road, Baden, PA 15005 US
724-266-2346; fax: 724-266-2346

Make Money Self-Publishing: Learn How from Fourteen Successful Small Publishers
By Suzanne P. Thomas (Gemstone House Publishing)
POB 19948, Boulder, CO 80308
800-324-6415

The Prepublishing Handbook:
What You Should Know Before You Publish Your First Book
By Patricia J. Bell (Cats Paw Press)
9561 Woodridge Circle, Eden Prairie, MN 55347
952-941-5053; fax: 952-941-4759; e-mailL catspawpress@aolcom

The Publish It Yourself Handbook (25th Anniversary Edition)
By Bill Henderson (Introduction): (W.W. Norton & Company)
500 Fifth Avenue, New York, NY 10110
212-354-5500

Publish Your Own Novel
By Connie Shelton, Lee Ellison, Editor (Intrigue Press)
POB 27553, Philadelphia, PA 19118
800-996-9783

Offical Contact Pages: Suggested Resources

The Self-Publishing's Writing Journal
By Lia Relova (Pumpkin Enterprises)
12 Packet Road, Palos Verdes, CA 90275
email: princesslia@hotmail.com

The Self-Publishing Manual: How to Write, Print & ell Your Own Book
By Dan Poynter (Para Publishing)
POB 8206-240, Santa Barbara, CA 93118-8206
805-968-7277; fax: 805-968-1379: celluar: 805-680-2298
e-mail: DanPoynter@aol.com,
75031.3534@compuserve.com.

A Simple Guide to Self-Publishing: A Step-by-Step Handbook to Prepare,
Print, Distribute & Promote Your Own Book – 3rd Edition
By Mark Ortman (Wise Owl Books)
POB 29205, Bellingham, WA 98228
360-671-5858: e-mail: publish@wiseowlbooks.com

Smart Self-Publishing: An Author's Guide to Produce a Marketable Book
By Linda G. Salisbury (Tabby House)
4429 Shady Lane, Charlotte Harbor, FL 33980-3024
941-629-7646; fax: 941-629-4270

The Woman's Guide to Self-Publishing
By Donna M. Murphy (Irie Publishing)
301 Boardwalk Drive, POB 273123, Ft. Collins, CO 80527-3123
970-482-4402; fax: 970-482-4402: e-mail: iriepub@verinet.com

INDUSTRY RESOURCES

30 Steps to Becoming a Writer and Getting Published:
The Complete Starter Kit for Aspiring Writers
By Scott Edelstein (Writers Digest Books)
1507 Dana Avenue, Cincinnati, OH 45207
513-531-222; fax: 513-531-4744

James Hickman

500 Ways to Beat the Hollywood Script Reader:
Writing the Screenplay the Reader Will Recommend
by Jennifer M. Lerch (Fireside)
1230 Avenue of the Americas, New York, NY 10020
212-698-7000

1001 Ways to Write Better $ Get Published
by Scott Edelstein (Writers Digest Books)
1507 Dana Avenue, Cincinnati, OH 45207
513-531-222; fax: 513-531-4744

Poet's Market: 1800 Places to Publish Your Poetry
By Nancy Breen; Editor (Writers Digest Books)
1507 Dana Avenue, Cincinnati, OH 45207
513-531-222; fax: 513-531-4744

Children's Writers & Illustrators Market
By Annie Bowling, Editor (Writers Digest Books)
1507 Dana Avenue, Cincinnati, OH 45207
513-531-2222; fax: 513-531-4744

Writer's Market: 8000 Editors Who Buy What You Write
(Electronic version also available.)
by Kirsten Holm, Editor (Writers Digest Books)
1507 Dana Avenue, Cincinnati, OH 45207
513-531-2222; fax: 513-531-4744

Advice to Writers: A Compendium of Quotes, Anecdotes,
and Writerly Wisdom
From a Dazzling Array of Literary Lights
By John Winoker, Compiler (Vintage Books)
299 Park Avenue, New York NY 10171
212-751-2600

The American Directory of Writer's Guidelines:
What Editors Want, What Editors Buy (3rd ed.)
By John C. Mutchler (Quill Driver Books)
1831 Industrial Way, #101, Sanger, CA 93657
fax: 559-876-2170; e-mail: sbm12@csufresno.edu

The Art and Science of Book Publishing
By Herbert S. Bailey Jr. (Ohio University Press)

Offical Contact Pages: Suggested Resources

Scott Quadrangle, Athens OH 45701

The Author's Guide to Marketing Your Books:
From Start to Success, for Writers and Publishers
By Don Best, Peter Goodman (Stone Bridge Press)
POB 8208, Berkeley, CA 94707
800-947-7271; fax: 510-524-8711: e-mail:
sbporter@stonebridge.com

An Author's Guide to Publishing
By Michael Legat (Robert Hale Ltd.)
Clerkenwell House 45-47, CLerkenwell Green , London,
England ECR1R 0HT
0171-251-2661

The Big Deal: Hollywood's Million-Dollar Spec Script Market
By Tome Taylor (William Morrow & Company)
1350 Avenue of the Americas, New York, NY 10019
212-261-6500

Book Blitz: Getting Your Book in the News: 60 Steps to a Best Seller
By Barbara Gaughen, Ernest Weckbaugh (Best Seller Books)
7456 Evergreen Drive, Santa Barbara, CA 93117
800-444-2524

Book Business: Publishing: Past, Present, and Future
By Jason Epstein (W.W. Norton & Company)
500 Fifth Avenue, New York NY 10110
212-354-5500; fax: 212-869-0856

Book Editors Talk to Writers
By Judy Mandell (John Wiley & Sons)
605 Third Avenue, New York, NY 10158-0012
212-850-6000; fax: 212-850-6088; e-mail:
info@wiley.com

Book Promotions for the Shameless:
101 Marketing Tips that Really Work (3.5 diskette)
by Lorna Tedder (Spilled Candy Publications)
POB 5202, Niceville, FL 32578-5202

850-897-4644; e-mail: orders@spilledcandy.com

The Book Publishing Industry
By Albert N. Greco (Ally & Bacon)
75 Arlington Street, Suite 300, Boston, MA 02116
617-848-6000

Book Publishing: The Basic Introduction
By John P. Dessauer (Continuum Publishing Group)
370 Lexington Avenue, New York, NY 10017
212-953-5858

Breaking into Print: How to Write and Publish Your First Book
By Jane L. Evanson, Luanne Dowling (Kendall/ Hunt Publishing Company)
4050 Westmark Drive, POB 1840, Dubuque, IA 52004-1840
800-228-0810, 319-589-1000

Business and Legal Forms for Authors and Self-Publishers
By Tad Crawford (Allworth Press)
10 East 23rd Street, New York, NY 10010
fax: 212-777-8261; e-mail: groberts@allworth.com

The Career Novelist: A Literary Agent Offers Strategies for Success
By Donald Maas (Heinemann)
22 Salmon Street, Port Melbourne, Victoria 3207, Australia
e-mail: customer@hi.com.au

The Case of Peter Rabbit: Changing Conditions of Literature for Children
By Margaret Mackey (Garland Publishing)
29 W. 35th Street, New York NY 10001-2299
212-216-7800; fax: 212-564-7854; e-mail:info@taylorandfrancis.com

Children's Writer's & Illustrator's Market, 2000: 800 Editors & Art Directors Who Buy Your Writing & Illustrations
by Alice Pope, Editor (Writers Digest Books)

Offical Contact Pages: Suggested Resources

1507 Dana Avenue, Cincinnati OH 45207
513-531-2222; fax: 513-531-4744

Complete Guide to Book Marketing
By David Cole (Allworth Press)
10 East 23rd Street, New York NY 10010
fax: 212-777-8261; e-mail: groberts@allworth.com

Complete Guide to Book Marketing
By David Cole (Allworth Press)
10 East 23rd Street, New York NY 10010
fax: 212-777-8261; e-mail: groberts@allworth.com

The Complete Guide to Book Publicity
By Jodee Blanco (Allworth Press)
10 East 23rd Street, Suite 210, New York NY 10010
212-777-8395

The Complete Guide to Writer's Groups, Conferences, and Workshops
By Eileen Malone (John Wiley & Sons)
605 Third Avenue, New York NY 10158-0012
212-850-6000; fax: 212-850-6088: e-mail: info@wiley.com

The Complete Guide to Writing Fiction and Nonfiction —— And Getting It Published
By Patricia Kubis, Robert Howland (Prentice Hall Direct)
240 Frisch Court, Paramus, NJ 07652
201-909-6200

A Complete Guide to Writing for Publication
By Susan Titus Osborn, Editor (ACW Press)
5501 N. 7th Ave., #502, Phoenix, AZ 85013
877-868-9673; e-mail: editor@acwpress.com

The Complete Idiot's Guide to Getting Your Romance Published
By Julie Beard (Alpha Books)
4500 E. Speedway, Suite 31, Tucson, AZ 85712
fax: 800-770-4329

The Copyright Permission and Libel Handbook:
A Step-by-Step Guide for Writers, Editors, and Publishers
By Lloyd J. Jassin, Steve C. Schecter (John Wiley & Sons)
605 Third Avenue, New York NY 10158-0012
212-850-6000; fax: 212-850-6088; e-mail:
info@wiley.com

Desktop Publishing & Design for Dummies
By Roger C. Parker (IDG Books Worldwide, Inc)
919 E. Hillsdale Blvd., Suite 400, Foster City CA 94404-2112
800-762-1974

Directory of Small Press/Magazine Editors & Publishers
(Directory of Small Press and Magazine Editors and Publishers, 31st Ed)
By Len Fulton, Editor (Dustbooks)
POB 100, Paradise CA 95967
530-877-6110, 800-477-6110; fax: 530-877-0222

Directory of Poetry Publishers 20th edition 2004-2005
By Len Fulton (Dustbooks)
POB 100, Paradise CA 95967
530-877-6110, 800-477-6110

Editors on Editing: What Writers Need to Know About What Editors Do
By Gerald Gross, Editor (Grove Press)
841 Broadway, New York NY 10003
212-614-7850

The First Five Pages: A Writer's Guide to Staying Out of the Rejection Pile
By Noah T. Lukeman (Fireside)
1230 Avenue of the Americas, New York, NY 10020
212-698-7000

Formatting & Submitting Your Manuscript (Writer's Market Library Series)
By Jack Neff (Writers Digest Books)
1507 Dana Avenue, Cincinnati OH 45207
513-531-2222; fax: 513-531-4744

Offical Contact Pages: Suggested Resources

From Book Idea to Bestseller: What You Absolutely, Positively Must Know To Make Your Book a Success
By Michael Snell, Kim Baker & Sunny Baker, Contributors
(Prima Publishing)
3000 Lava Ridge Court, Roseville, CA 95661

From Pen to Print: the Secrets of Getting Published Successfully
By Ellen M. Kozak (Henry Holt)
115 West 18th Street, New York, NY 10011
212-886-9200; fax: 212-633-0748: e-mail: publicity@hholt.com

Get Published: Top Magazine Editors Tell You How
By Diane Gage (Henry Holt)
115 West 18th Street, New York NY 10011
212-886-9200; fax: 212-633-0748; e-mail:publicity@hholt.com

Get Your First Book Published: And Make It a Success
By Jason Shinder, Jeff Herman, Amy Holman (Career Press)
3 Tice Road, POB 687, Franklin Lakes, NJ 07417
201-848-0310

Getting Your Book Published for Dummies
By Sarah Parsons Zackheim (IDG Books Worldwide, Inc.)
919 E. Hillsdale Blvd. Suite 400, Foster City, CA 94404-2112
800-762-2974

Getting Your Manuscript Sold: Surefire Writing and Selling Strategies
That Will Get Your Book Published
By Cynthia Sterling, M. G. Davidson (Empire Publishing Service)
POB 717, Madison, NC 27025-0717
Fax: 336-427-7372

How to Be Your Own Literary Agent: The Business of Getting a Book Published

By Richard Mariotti and Bruce Fife (Piccadilly Books)

How to Get Happily Published (5th Ed.)
By Judith Appelbaum (HarperCollins)
10 East 53rd Street, New York NY 10022-5299
212-207-7000

How to Publish, Promote, and Sell Your Own Book
By Robert Lawrence Holt (St. Martin's Press)
175 Fifth Avenue, New York NY 10010
212-674-5151

How to Write a Book Proposal
By Michael Larsen (Writers Digest Books)
1507 Dana Avenue, Cincinnati OH 45207
513-531-2222; fax: 513-531-4744

How to Write a Damn Good Novel
By James N. Frey (St. Martin's Press)
175 Fifth Avenue, New York, NY 10010
212-674-5151

How to Write and Sell Your First Nonfiction Book
By Oscar Collier, Frances Spatz Leighton (St. Martin's Press)
175 Fifth Avenue, New York NY 10010
212-674-5151

How to Write Irresistible Query Letters
By Lisa Collier Cool (Writers Digest Books)
1507 Dana Avenue, Cincinnati OH 45207
513-531-2222; fax: 513-531-4744

How To Write Killer Fiction
By Carolyn Wheat (Perseverance Press)

How to Write What You Want and Sell What You Write
By Skip Press (Career Press)
3 Tice Road POB 687, Franklin Lakes, NJ 07417
201-848-0310

Immediate Fiction: A Complete Writing Course

Offical Contact Pages: Suggested Resources

By Jerry Cleaver (St. Martin's Press)

In the Company of Writers: A Life in Publishing
By Charles Scribner (Scribner)
1230 Avenue of the Americas, New York NY 10020
212-698-7000

The Insider's Guide to Getting an Agent
By Lori Perkins (Writers Digest Books)
1507 Dana Avenue, Cincinnati OH 45207
513-531-2222; fax: 513-531-4744

The Joy of Publishing
By Nat G. Bodian (Open Horizons)
POB 205, Fairfield, IA 52556

Jump Start Your Book Sales: A Money-Making Guide for Authors,
Independent Publishers and Small Presses
By Marilyn Ross, Tom Ross (Writers Digest Books)
1507 Dana Avenue, Cincinnati, OH 45207
513-531-2222; fax: 513-531-4744

Kirsch's Guide to the Book Contract: For Authors, Publishers, Editors and Agents
By Jonathan Kirsch (Acrobat Books)
POB 870, Venice, CA 90294
Fax: 310-823-8447

Kirsch's Handbook of Publishing Law: For Author's Publishers, Editors, and Agents
By Jonathan Kirsch (Acrobat Books)
POB 870, Venice, CA 90294
Fax: 310-823-8447

Literary Agents: The Essential Guide for Writers
By Debby Mayer (Penguin Books)

Literary Agents: What They Do, How They Do It, and How to Find And Work with the right One for You, Revised and Expanded
By Michael Larsen (John Wiley & Sons)

605 Third Avenue, New York NY 10158-0012
212-850-6000; fax: 212-850-6088; e-mail:
info@wiley.com

Literary Marketplace 2001: The Directory of the American Book Publishing Industry with Industry Yellow Pages
By R.R. Bowker Staff (R.R. Bowker)
630 Central Avenue, New Providence NJ 07974
888-269-5372; e-mail: info@bowker.com

Making It in Book Publishing
By Leonard Mogal (IDG Books Worldwide, Inc)
919 E. Hillside Blv. Ste. 400, Foster City, CA 94404-2112
800-762-2974

Marketing Strategies for Writers
By Michael H. Sedge (Allworth Press)
10 East 23rd Street, Ste. 210, New York NY 10010
212-777-8395

Merriam-Webster's Manual for Writers and Editors
Merriam Webster
47 Federal Street, POB 281 Springfield, MA 01102
413-734-3134; fax 413-731-5979; e-mail: mwsales@m-w.com

Negotiating a Book contract: A Guide for Authors, Agents and Lawyers
By Mark L. Levine (Moyer Bell Ltd.)
Kymbole Way, Wakefield, RI 02879
401-789-0074, 888-789-1945; fax: 401-789-3793
e-mail: sales@moyerbell.com

Nonfiction Book Proposals Anybody Can Write: How to Get a Contract and Advance Before Writing Your Book
By Elizabeth Lyon (Blue Heron Pub)
1234 SW Stark Street, Ste. 1, Portland, OR 97205
fax: 503-223-9474: e-mail: bhp@teleport.com

Novel & Short Story Writer's Market, 2005: 2000 Places to Sell Your Fiction

Offical Contact Pages: Suggested Resources

(Novel and Short Story Writer's Market, 2000)
by Barbara Kuroff & Tricia Waddell, Editors (Writers Digest Books)
1507 Dana Avenue, Cincinnati OH 45207
fax: 531-531-4744

The Plot Thickens: 8 Ways to Bring Fiction to Life
By Noah Lukeman (St. Martin's Press)

Poet Power! The Practical Poet's Complete Guide to Getting Published (and Self-Published)
By Thomas A. Williams (Venture Press)
POB 1582, Davis, CA 95617-1582
530-756-2309; fax: 530-756-4790; e-mail: wmaster@ggweb.com

The Portable Writers' Conference: Your Guide to Getting and Staying Published
By Stephen Blake Mettee, Editor (Word Dancer Press)
1831 Industrial Way, #101, Sanger, CA 93657
voice/fax: 559-876-2170; e-mail: sbm@csufresno.edu

The Prepublishing Handbook: What You Should Know Before You Publish Your First Book
By Patricia J. Bell (Cats Paw Press)
9561 Woodridge Circle, Eden Prairie, MN 55347
952-941-5053; fax: 952-941-4759; email: catspawpre@aol.com

Publish to Win: Smart Strategies to Sell More Books
By Jerrold R. Jenkins, Anne M. Stanton (Rhodes & Easton)
35 Clark Hill Road, Prospect CT 06712-1011
203-758-3661; fax: 603-853-5420; e-mail: biopub@aol.com

The Screenwriter's Bible: A Complete Guide to Writing, Formatting and Selling Your Script
By David Trottier (Silman-James Press)
3624 Shannon RD, Los Angeles CA 90027
323-661-9922; fax: 323-661-9933

Secrets of a Freelance Writer: How to Make $85,000 a Year
By Robert W. Bly (Henry Holt)
115 West 18th St. New York, NY 10011
212-886-9200; fax: 212-633-0748; e-mail: publicity@hholt.com

Self-Editing for Fiction Writer
By Renni Browne, Dave King (HarperCollins)
10 East 53rd ST. New York, NY 10022-5299
212-207-7000

A Simple Guide to Marketing Your Book:
What an Author and Publisher Can do to Sell More Books
By Mark Ortman (Wise Owl Books)
24425 Fieldmont Place, West Hills, CA 91307
818-716-9076; e-mail: apweis@pacbell.net

The Shortest Distance Between You and a Published Book
By Susan Page (Broadway Books)
841 Broadway, New York, NY 10003
212-614-7850

Telling Lies for Fun & Profit
By Lawrence Block, Sue Grafton (Introduction); (William Morrow & Company)
1350 Avenue of the Americas, New York, NY 10019
212-261-6500

This Business of Books: A Complete Overview of the Industry from Concept Through Sales
By Claudia Suzanne, Carol Amato & Thelma Sansoucie, Editors (Wambtac)
17300 17th Street, #J276, Tustin, CA 92780
800-641-3936; fax: 714-954-0793; e-mail: bookdoc@wambtac

This Business of Publishing: An Insider's View of Current Trends and Tactics
By Richard Curtis (Allworth Press)
10 East 23rd Street, Ste. 210, New York, NY 10010
212-777-8395

Offical Contact Pages: Suggested Resources

What Book Publishers Won't Tell You
A Literary Agent's Guide to the Secrets of Getting Published
By Bill Adler (Citadel Press)
3300 Business Dr., Sacramento, CA 95820
fax: 916-732-2070

The Whole Picture: Strategies for Screenwriting Success in the New Hollywood
By Richard Walter (Plume)
375 Hudson St., New York, NY 10014
212-366-2000

Writer Tells All: Insider Secrets to Getting Your Book Published
By Robert Masello (Owl Books)
115 West 18th St., New York, NY 10010
212-886-9200

Write the Perfect Book Proposal: 10 Proposals That Sold and Why
By Jeff Herman, Deborah M. Adams (John Wiley & Sons)
605 Third Avenue, New York, NY 10158-0012
212-850-6000; fax: 212-850-6088; e-mail:
info@wiley.com

A Writer's Guide to Overcoming Rejection
A Practical Sales Course for the As Yet Unpublished
By Edward Baker (Summerdale Publishing Ltd.)

Writer's International Guide to Book Editors, Publishers, and Literary Agents:
Make the Whole English-Speaking Publishing World Yours with This One-of-a-Kind Guide
By Jeff Herman (Prima Publishing)
3000 Lava Ridge Court, Roseville, CA 95661

The Writer's Market Companion
By Joe Feiertag, Mary Carmen Cupito (Writer's Digest Books)
1507 Dana Ave. Cincinatti, OH 45207
513-531-2222; fax: 531-531-4744

Writer's & Illustrator's Guide to Children's Book Publishers and Agents
By Ellen R. Shapiro (Prima Publishing)
3000 Lava Ridge Ct., Roseville, CA 95661

The Writer's Legal Companion: The Complete Handbook for the Working Writer
By Brad Bunnin, Peter Beren (Perseus Press)
11 Cambridge Center, Cambridge, MA 02142
e-mail: info@perseuspublishing.com

The Writer's Legal Guide (2nd ed.)
By Tad Crawford, Tony Lyons (Allworth Press)
10 East 23rd St. Ste. 210, New York, NY 10010
212-777-8395

The Writer's Little Instruction Book: 385 Secrets for Writing Well and Getting Published
By Paul Raymond Martin, Polly Keener (Writer's World Press)
35 N. Chillecothe Rd. Ste. D, Aurora, OH 44202
330-562-6667; fax: 330-562-1216; e-mail: Writersworld@juno.com

Official contact pages. Self-Publishing& marteting
By James Hickman (bent Publishing)
5441 Riverdale Rd#129 College park,GA 30349
404-246-6496 www.bentpublishing.com

Writing Down the Bones: Freeing the Writer Within
By Natalie Goldberg (Shambhala Publications)
POB 308, Boston, MA 02117
617-424-0030; fax: 617-236-1563

Writing Successful Self-Help and How-To-Books
By Jean Marie Stine (John Wiley & Sons)
605 Third Avenue, New York, NY 10158-0012
212-850-6000; fax: 212-850-6088; e-mail: info@wiley.com

Writing the Nonfiction Book

Offical Contact Pages: Suggested Resources

By Eva Shaw, Ph.D. (Rodgers & Nelsen Publishing Company)
POB 700, Loveland, CO 80537
970-593-9557

You Can Make It Big Writing Books:
A Top Agent Shows How to Develop A Million-Dollar Bestseller
By Jeff Herman, Deborah Levine Herman, Julia DeVillers
(Prima Publishing)
3000 Lava Ridge Ct. Roseville, CA 95661

Your Novel Proposal: From Creation to Contract: The Complete Guide to
Writing Query Letters, Synopses and Proposals for Agents and Editors
By Blythe Camenson (Writers Digest Books)
1507 Dana Avenue, Cincinnati, OH 45207
513-531-2222; fax; 513-531-4744

E-PUBLISHING RESOURCES

A Cheap and Easy Guide to Digital Publishing
By William E. Kasdorf (Columbia University Press)

Electronic Books and Epublishing: A Practical Guide for Authors
By Harold Henke (Springer Verlag)

Electronic Publishing: The Definitive Guide
By Karen S. Wiesner (Avid Press)
5470 Red Fox Dr., Brighton, MI 48114
810-801-1177; e-mail: cgs@avidpress.com

EBook Marketing Made Easy
By Rusty Fisher (Bookbooters.com)

ePublishing for Dummies
By Victoria Rosenborg (Hungry Minds, Inc.)
909 Third Avenue, New York, NY 10022

The Freelance Writer's E-Publishing Guidebook: 25+ E-Publishing Home-Based
Online Writing Businesses to Start for Freelancers
By Anne Hart (iUniverse.com)
800-375-1736; e-mail: publisher@iuniverse.com

How to Get Your E Book Published
By Richard Curtis, W. T. Quick (Writers Digest Books)
1507 Dana Ave. Cincinnati, OH 45207
513-531-2222; fax: 513-531-4744

How to Publish and Promote Online
By M.J. Rose Angela Adair-Hoy (Griffin Trade Paperback)
175 Fifth Avenue, New York, NY 10010
212-647-5151

Official Adobe Electronic Publishing Guide
By Adobe Creative Team (Adobe Press)
345 Park Avenue, San Jose, CA 95110-2704
408-536-6000

Poor Richard's Creating eBooks
By Chris Van Buren, Jeff Cogswell, Matt Wagner (top Floor Publishing)

Real ePublishing, Really Publishing!: How to Create Digital Books by and for All Ages
By Mark W.F. Condon and Michael Mcguffee (Heinmann)

U-Publish.com: How Individual Writers Can Now Effectively Compete
With the Giants of Publishing
By Dan Snow, Danny O. Poynter (Unlimited Publishing)
POB 3007, Bloomington, IN 47402
e-mail: publish@unlimitedpublishing.com

*What Every Writer *Must* Know About E-Publishing*
By Emily A. Vander Veer (Emil A. Vander Veer)
e-mail: Emily@emilyv.com

Offical Contact Pages: Suggested Resources

Writing.Com: Creative Internet Strategies to Advance Your Writing Career
By Moira Anderson Allen (Allworth Press)
10 East 23rd St., Ste. 210, New York, NY 10010
212-777-8395

Your Guide to Ebook Publishing Success:
How to Create and Profitably Sell Your Writing on the Internet
By James Dillehay (Warm Snow Publishers)
50 Sufi Rd., POB 75, Torreon, NM 87061
e-mail: service@craftmarketer.com

10. GLOSSARY

A

abstract A brief sequential profile of chapters in a nonfiction book proposal (also called a synopsis); a point-by-point summary of an article or essay. In academic and technical journals, abstracts often appear with (and may serve to preface) the articles themselves.

adaptation A rewrite or reworking of a piece for another medium, such as the adaptation of a novel for the screen.

advance Money paid (usually in installments) to an author by a publisher prior to publication. The advance is paid against royalties: If an author is given a $5000 advance, for instance, the author will collect royalties only after the royalty money due exceed $5000 advance, for instance, the author will collect royalties only after the money due exceed $5000. A good contract protects the advance if it should exceed the royalties ultimately due from sales.

advance orders Orders received before a book's official publication date, and sometimes before actual completion of the book's production and manufacture.

agent The person who acts on behalf of the author to handle the sale of the author's literary properties. Good literary agents are as valuable to publishers as they are to writers; they select and present manuscripts appropriate for particular houses or of interest to particular acquisitions editors. Agents are paid on a percentage basis from the moneys due their author clients.

American Booksellers Association (ABA) The major trade organization for retail book-sellers, chain and independent. The annual ABA convention and trade show offers a chance for publishers and distributors to display their wares to the industry at large and provides an incomparable networking forum for booksellers, editors, agents, publicists, and authors.

American Society of Journalists and Authors (ASJA) A membership organization for professional writers, ADJA provides a forum for information exchange among writers and other s in the publishing community, as well as networking opportunities.

anthology A collection of stories, poems, essays and/ or selections from larger works (and so forth), usually carrying a unifying theme or concept; these selections may be written by different authors or by single author, Anthologies are compiled as opposed to written; their editors (as opposed to authors) are responsible for securing the needed reprint rights for the material used, as well as supplying (or providing authors for) pertinent introductory or supplementary material and/or commentary.

attitude A contemporary colloquialism used to describe a characteristic temperament common among individuals who consider themselves superior. Attitude is rarely an esteemed attribute, whether in publishing or elsewhere.

auction Manuscripts a literary agent believes to be hot properties (such as possible bestsellers with strong subsidiary rights potential) will be offered for confidential bidding from multiple publishing houses. Likewise, the reprint, film, and other rights to a successful book may be auctioned off by the original publisher's subsidiary rights or by the author's agent.

audio books Works produced for distribution on audio media, typically audiotape cassette or audio compact disc (CD), Audio books are usually spoken-word adaptations of works originally created and produced in print; these works sometimes feature the author's own voice; many are given dramatic reading s by one or more actors, at times embellished with sound effects.

authorized biography A history of a person's life written with the authorization, cooperation, and at times, participation of the subject or the subject's heirs.

author's copies/ author's discount Author's copies are the free copies of the books the authors receive from the publisher; the exact number is stipulated in the contract, but it is usually at least 10 hardcovers. The author will be able to purchase more copies of the book (usually at 40% discount from retail price) and resell them at readings, lectures, and other public engagements. In cases where large quantities of books are bought, author discounts can go as high as 70%.

author tour A series of travel and promotional appearances by an author on behalf of the author's book.

autobiography A historical account of a person's life written by that person, or as typical composed conjointly with a collaborative writer or ghostwriter. Autobiographies by definition entail the authorization, cooperation, participation, and ultimate approval of the subject.

B

backlist The backlist comprises books published prior to the current season and still in print. Traditionally, at some publishing houses, such backlist titles represent the publisher's cash flow mainstays. Some backlist books continue to sell; some remain bestsellers over several successive seasons; others sell slowly but surely through they years. Although many backlist titles may be difficult to find in bookstores that stock primarily current lists, they can be ordered either through a local bookseller or directly from the publisher.

backmatter Elements of a book that follow the text proper. Backmatter may include the appendix, notes, glossary, bibliography and other references, list of resources, index, author, biography, offerings of the author's and/ or publisher's additional books and other related merchandise, and colophon.

bestseller Based on sales or orders by bookstores, wholesalers, and distributors, bestsellers are those titles that move the largest quantities. List of bestselling books can be local (as in metropolitan newspapers), regional, or national (as in USA Today, Publishers Weekly, or the New York Times), as well as international. Fiction and nonfiction are usually listed separately, as are hardcover and paperback classifications. Depending on the list's purview, additional industry-sector designations are used (such as how-to/ self-improvement, religion and spirituality, business and finance); in addition, bestseller lists can be keyed to particular genre or specialty fields (such as bestseller lists for mysteries, science fiction, or romance novels, and for historical works, biography, or popular science titles) – and virtually any other marketing category at the discretion of whoever issues the bestseller list. (for instance African-American interests, and youth markets.)

bibliography A list of books, articles, and other sources, that have been used in the writing of the text in which the bibliography appears.

binding The materials that hold a book together (including the cover). Bindings are generally denoted as hardcover or paperback.

biography A history of a person's life.

blues (or bluelines) Photographic proofs of the printing plates for a book. Blues are reviewed as a means to inspect the set type, layout, and design of the books pages before it goes to press.

blurb A piece of written copy or extracted quotation used for publicity and promotional purposes, as on a flyer, in a catalog, or in an advertisement.

book club A book club is a book-marketing operation that ships selected titles to subscribing members on a regular basis, sometimes at greatly reduced prices. Sales of a work to a book club are handled through the publisher's subsidiary rights department.

book contract A legally binding document between author and publisher that sets the terms for the advance, royalties, subsidiary rights, advertising, promotion, publicity, - plus a host of other contingencies and responsibilities.

book distribution The method of getting books from the publisher's warehouse into reader's hands. Distribution is mostly through bookstores but can include telemarketing, mail-order and a variety of special interest outlets.

book producer An individual or company that can assume many of the roles in the publishing process. They may conceive the idea for a book or series, bring together the professional needed to make the book, sell the individual manuscript or series project to a publisher, take the project through to manufactured product – or perform any selection of those functions, as commissioned by the publisher or other client. The book producer may have separate contracts with the publishers, writers, or illustrators.

book review A critical appraisal of a book that evaluates such aspects as organization and writing style, possible market appeal, and cultural, political, or literary significance.

Books in Print Listings, published by R.R. Bowker of books currently in print; these yearly volumes provide ordering information, including titles, authors, ISBN numbers, prices, whether the book is available in hardcover or paperback, and publisher names. Intended for use by the book trade, it can be a great marketing resource for writers.

bound galleys Copies of uncorrected typesetter's page proofs or printouts of electronically produced mechanicals that are bound together as advance copies of the book.

Offical Contact Pages: Glossary

bulk sales The sale at a set discount of many copies of a single title (the greater the number of books, the lager the discount.

byline The name of the author of a given piece, indicating credit for having written a book or article.

C

casing Alternate term for binding.

category fiction Also known as genre fiction. Category fiction falls into established marketing category. Fiction categories include action-adventure, crime novels, mysteries/detective fiction, romances, horror, thrillers, Westerns, science fiction, and fantasy.

CD or computer CD High capacity discs for use by reader via computer technology.

children's books Books for children. Defined by the book publishing industry, children are generally readers aged 17 and younger; many houses adhere to a fine but firm editorial distinction between titles intended for younger readers.

coauthor One who shares authorship of a work. Coauthors all have bylines. Coauthor share royalties based on their contributions to the book.

collaboration Writers can collaborate with professionals in any number of fields. Often a writer can collaborate in order to produce books outside the writer's own areas of formally credentialed expertise.

colophon Strictly speaking a colophon is a publisher's logo; in bookmaking the term may also refer to a listing of the materials used, as well as credits for the design, composition, and production of the book.

commercial fiction Fiction written to appeal to as broad-based a readership as possible.

concept A general statement for the idea behind a book.

cooperative advertising (co-op) An agreement between a publisher and a bookstore. The publisher's book is featured in an ad for the bookstore.

copublishing Joint publishing of a book, usually by a publisher and another corporate entity. An author can copublish with the publisher by sharing costs, decision making, and profits.

copyeditor An editor, responsible for the final polishing of a manuscript, who reads primarily in terms of appropriate word usage and grammatical expression, with an eye toward clarity and coherence of the material as presented, factual error and inconsistencies, spelling, and punctuation.

copyright The legal proprietary right to reproduce, have reproduced, publish, and sell copies of literary, musical, and other artistic works. The rights to literary properties reside in the author from the time the work is produced—regardless of whether a formal copyright registration is obtained. However, for legal reasons in the event of plagiarism or other infringement, the work must be registered with the U.S. Copyright Office, and all copies of the work must bear the copyright notice.

cover blurbs Favorable quotes from other writers, celebrities, or experts in a book's subject area, which appear on the dust jacket and are used to enhance the book's point-of-purchase appeal to the potential book-buying public.

crash Coarse gauze used in bookbinding to strengthen the spine and joints of a book.

curriculum vitae (c.v.) Latin expression meaning "course of life" – in other words, the resume.

D

deadline In book publishing, this is used for the author's due date for delivery of the completed manuscript to the publisher.

delivery Submission of the complete manuscript to the publisher.

Dial-a-Writer Members of the American Society of Journalists and Authors may be listed with the organization's project-referral service, Dial-a-Writer, which can provide accomplished writers in most specialty fields and subjects.

direct marketing Advertising that involves a "direct response" from a consumer.

display titles Books that are produced to be eye-catching to the casual shopper in a bookstore setting.

distributor An agent or business that buys books from a publisher to resell, at a higher cost, to wholesalers, retailers, or individuals.

dramatic rights Legal permission to adapt a work for the stage. These rights initially belong to the author but can be sold or assigned to another party by the author.

dust jacket The wrapper that covers the binding of hardcover books, designed especially for the book by either the publisher's art department or a freelance artist.

dust-jacket copy Descriptions of books printed on the dust-jacket flaps.

E

editor Editorial responsibilities and titles vary from house to house. In general, the duties of the editor-in-chief are primarily administrative; managing personnel, scheduling, budgeting, and defining the editorial personality of the firm or imprint.

Editorial Freelancers Association (EFA) This organization of independent professionals offers a referral service, through both its annotated membership directory and its job phone line, as a means for authors and publishers to connect with writers, collaborators, researchers, and a wide range of editorial experts covering virtually all general and specialist fields.

el-hi Books for elementary and/ or high schools.

endnotes Explanatory notes and/or source citations that appear either at the end of individual chapters or at the end of a book's text; used primarily in scholarly or academically oriented works.

epilogue The final segment of a book which comes after "the end".

F

fantasy Fantasy is fiction that features elements or magic, wizardry, supernatural feats, and entities that suspend conventions of realism in the literary arts. Fantasy can resemble prose versions of epics and rhymes or it may informed by mythic cycles or folkloric material derived from cultures worldwide.

film rights Like dramatic rights , these belong to the author, who may sell or option them to someone in the film industry.

footnotes Explanatory notes and/or source citations that appear at the bottom of a page.

Offical Contact Pages: Glossary

foreign agents   Persons who work with their U.S. counterparts to acquire rights for books from the U.S. for publication abroad.

foreign market Any foreign entity—a publisher, broadcast mediums, etc. in a position to buy rights. Authors share royalties with whoever negotiates the deal or keep 100% if they do their own negotiating.

foreign rights   Translation or reprint rights that can be sold abroad. Foreign rights belong to the author but can be sold either country-by-country or en masse as world rights.

foreword   An introductory piece written by the author or by an expert in the given field.

Frankfurt Book Fair   The largest international publishing exhibition with 500 years of tradition behind it. It takes place every year in Frankfurt, Germany.

Freedom of Information Act   Ensures the protection of the public's right to access public records- except in cases violating the right to privacy, national security, or certain other instances.

freight passthrough   The bookseller's freight cost. (the cost of getting the book from the publisher to the bookseller)

frontlist   New titles published in a given season by a publisher. Frontlist usually get priority exposure in the front of the sales catalog.

frontmatter   The elements that precede the text of the work, such as the title page, shipping, receiving returns, and mail-order and direct-marketing functions.

G

galleys   Printer's proofs on sheets of paper, or printouts of the electronically produced setup of the books' interior.

ghostwriter   A writer without a byline, often without the remuneration and recognition that credited authors receive.

glossary   An alphabetical listing of special terms as they are used in a particular subject area.

H

hardcover   Books bound in a format that uses thick, sturdy, stiff binding boards and a cover composed of a cloth spine and finished binding paper.

headbands   Thin strips of cloth that adorn the top of a book's spine where the signatures are held together.

hook   A term denoting the distinctive concept or theme of a work that sets it apart as being fresh, new, or different from others in its field.

horror   The horror classification denotes works that traffic in the bizarre, awful, and scary in order to entertain as well as explicate the darkness at the heart of the reader's soul.

how-to books   An immensely popular category of books ranging from purely instructional to motivational, to get rich quick.

hypertext   Works in hypertext are meant to be more than words and other images. These productions are conceived to take advantage of readers' and writers' propensities to seek out twists in narrative trajectories and to bushwhack from the main path of multifaceted reference topics.

I

imprint A separate line of product within a publishing house. Imprints run the gamut or complexity, from those composed of one or two series to those offering full-fledged and diversified lists.

index An alphabetical directory at the end of a book that references names and subjects discussed in the book and the pages where such mentions can be found.

instant book A book produced quickly to appear in bookstores as soon as possible after a newsworthy event to which it is relevant.

international copyright Rights secured for countries that are members of the International Copyright Convention.

International Copyright Convention Countries that are signatories to the various international copyright treaties.

introduction Preliminary remarks pertaining to a piece. Like a foreword, an introduction can be written by the author or an appropriate authority on the subject.

ISBN (International Standard Book Number) A 10-digit number that is linked to and identifies the title and publisher of a book. It is used for ordering and cataloging books and appears on all dust jackets, on the back cover, and the copyright page.

ISSN (International Standard Serial Number) An 8-digit cataloging and ordering number that identifies all U.S. and foreign periodicals.

K

kill fee   A fee paid by a magazine when it cancels a commissioned article. The fee is only a certain percentage of the agreed –on payment for the assignment.

L

lead   The crucial first few sentences, phrases, or words of anything—be it query letter, proposal, novel, news release, advertisement, or sales tip sheet.

lead title   A frontlist book featured by the publisher during a given season. One the publisher thinks will be a commercial success.

letterhead   Business stationary and envelopes imprinted with the company's name, address, and logo.

letterpress   A form of printing in which set type is linked, then impressed directly onto the printing surface.

libel   Defamation of an individual(s) in a published work, with malice aforethought. In litigation, the falsity of the libelous statements or representations, as well as the intention of malice, has to be proved for there to be libel.

Library of Congress (LOC)   The largest library in the world is in D.C. As part of its many services, the LOC will supply a writer with up-to-date sources and bibliographies in all fields.

Library of Congress Catalog Number   An identifying number issued by the Library of Congress to books it has accepted for its collection.

Literary Market Place LMP   Annual directory of the publishing industry that contains a comprehensive list of publisher, alphabetically and by category, with their addresses and phone numbers.

Offical Contact Pages: Glossary

literature   Written works of fiction and nonfiction in which compositional excellence and advancement in the art of writing are higher priorities than are considerations of profit or commercial appeal.

logo   A company or product identifier; for example, a representation of a company's initials or a drawing that is the exclusive property of that company.

M

mainstream fiction   Nongenre fiction, excluding literary or avant-garde fiction, that appeals to a general readership.

marketing plan   The entire strategy for selling a book: its publicity, promotion, sales, and advertising.

mass-market paperback   Less-expensive smaller-format paperbacks that are sold from rack as well as in bookstores.

mechanicals   Typeset copy and art mounted on boards to be photocopied and printed.

midlist books   Generally mainstream fiction and nonfiction books that traditionally formed the bulk of a publisher's list.

multimedia   Presentations of sound and light, words in magnetically graven image- and any known combination thereof as well as nuances yet to come.

multiple contract   A book contract that includes a provisional agreement for a future book or books.

N

net receipts The amount of money a publisher actually receives for sales of a book: the retail price minus the bookseller's discount and/or other discount.

New Age An eclectic category that encompasses health, medicine, philosophy, religion, and the occult- presented from an alternative or multicultural perspective.

novella A work of fiction falling in length between a short story and a novel.

O

offset (offset lithography) A printing process that involves the transfer of wet ink from a printing plate onto an intermediate surface and then onto the paper.

option clause/ right of first refusal In a book contract, a clause that stipulates that the publisher will have the exclusive right to consider and make an offer for th e author's next book.

outline Used for both a book proposal and the actual writing and structuring of a book, an outline is hierarchical listing of topics that provides the writer with an overview of the ideas in a book in the order in which they will be presented.

out-of-print books Books no longer available from the publisher; rights usually revert to the author.

P

package The package is the actual book. The physical product.

Offical Contact Pages: Glossary

page proof   The final typeset copy of the book, n page-layout form, before printing.

paperback originals   Books published, generally in paperback editions only; sometimes the term refers to those books publisher simultaneously in hardcover and paperback.

permissions   The right to quote or reprint published material, obtained by the author form the copyright holder.

picture book   A copiously illustrated book, often with very simple, limited text, intended for preschoolers and very young children.

plagiarism   The false presentation of someone else's writing as one's own.

preface   An element of a book's frontmatter. The author may discuss the purpose behind the format of the book, the type of research upon which it is based, its genesis, or underlying philosophy.

premium   Books sold at a reduced price as part of a special promotion. Premiums can be sold to the bookseller which in turn sells them to the bookbuyer .

press kit   A promotional package that includes a press release, tip sheet, author biography and photograph, review, and other pertinent information.

price   There are several prices pertaining to a single book: the invoice price is the amount the publisher charges the bookseller; the retail, cover, or list price is what the consumer pays.

printer's error (PE)   A typographical error made by the printer or typesetting facility, not by the publisher's staff. PE's are corrected at the printer's expense.

printing plate   A surface that bears a reproduction of the set type and artwork of a book, form which the pages are printed.

proposal   A detailed presentation of the book's concept, used to gain the interest and services of an agent and to sell the project to a publisher.

public domain   Material that is uncopyrighted, whose copyright has expired, or that is uncopyrightable. The last includes government publications, jokes, title- and ideas.

publication date (pub date)   A book's official date of publication, customarily set by the publisher to fall 6 weeks after completed bound books are delivered to the warehouse.

publicist (press agent)   The publicity professional who handles the press release for books and arranges the author's publicity tours and other promotional venues.

publisher's catalog   A seasonal sales catalog that lists and describes a publisher's new books; it is sent to all potential buyers, including individuals who request one.

publisher's discount   The percentage by which a publisher discounts the retail price of a book to a bookseller, often based in part on the number of copies purchased.

Publisher's Trade List Annual   A collection of current and backlist catalogs arranged alphabetically by publisher.

Publishers Weekly (PW)   The publishing industry's chief trade journal. PW carries announcement of upcoming books, respected book reviews, interviews with authors and publishing-industry professionals, special reports on various book categories, and trade news.

Q

quality   In publishing parlance, the word "quality" in reference to a book category of format is a tram or art- individual works or lines so described are presented as outstanding products.

query letter   A brief written presentation to an agent or editor designed to pitch both the writer and the book idea.

R

remainders   Unsold book stock. Remainders can include titles that have not sold as well as anticipated, in addition to unsold copies of later printings of bestsellers.

reprint   A subsequent edition of material that is already in print, especially publication in a different format- the paperback reprint of a hardcover, for example.

resume   A summary of an individual's career experience and education. When sent to agents and publishers, it should have the author's publishing credits, specialty credentials, and pertinent personal experience.

returns   Unsold books returned to a publisher by a bookstore, for which the store may receive full or partial credit.

reversion-of-rights clause   In the book contract, a clause that states that if the book goes out of print or the publisher fails to reprint the book within a stipulated length of time, all rights revert to the author.

review copy   A free copy of a new book sent to electronic and print media that review books for their audiences.

romance fiction or romance novels   Modern or period love stories, always with happy endings, which range from the tepid to the torrid.

royalty   The percentage of the retail cost of a book that is paid to the author for each copy sold after the author's advance has been recouped.

S

sales conference A meeting of publisher's editorial and sales departments and senior promotion and publicity staff member. It covers the upcoming season's new books and marketing strategies are discussed.

sales representative A member of the publisher's sales force or an independent contractor who, armed with a book catalog and order forms, visits bookstores in a certain territory to sell books to retailers.

SASE (self-addressed stamped envelope) It is customary for an author to enclose SASEs with query letter, with proposals, and with manuscript submissions.

satisfactory clause In book contracts, a publisher will reserve the right to refuse publication of a manuscript that is not satisfactory. Because the author may be forced to pay back the publisher's advance if the complete work is found to be unsatisfactory, the specific criteria for publisher satisfaction should be set forth in the contract to protect the author.

science fiction Includes the hardcore, imaginatively embellished technological/ scientific novel as well as fiction that is even slightly futuristic.

science fiction/ fantasy A category fiction designation that actually collapses two genres into one.

screenplay A film script- either original or one based on material publisher previously in another form, such as a television docudrama based on a nonfiction book or a movie thriller based on a suspense novel.

Offical Contact Pages: Glossary

self-publishing   A publishing project wherein an author pays for the costs of manufacturing and selling his or her own book and retains all the money from the book's sale.

self-syndication   Management by writers or journalists of functions that are otherwise performed by syndicates specializing in such services.

serial rights   Reprint rights sold to periodicals. First serial rights include the right to publish the materials before anyone else.

serialization   The reprinting of a book or part of a book in a newspaper or magazine. Serialization before the publication of the book is call first serial.

series   Books published as a group either because of their related subject matter and/ or single authorship.

shelf life   The amount of time an unsold book remains on the bookstore shelf before the manager pulls it from the shelf to make room for a book with more sales potential.

short story   A brief piece of fiction that is more pointed and more economically detailed as to character, situation, and plot than a novel.

signature   A group of book pages that have been printed together on one large sheet of paper that is then folded and cut in preparation for being bound, along with the book's other signatures, into the final volume.

simultaneous publication   The issuing at the same time of more than one edition of a work, such as in hardcover and trade paperback.

simultaneous (or multiple) submissions   The submission of the same material to more than one publisher at the same time. Although this is a common practice, publishers should always be aware that it is being done.

slush pile   The morass of unsolicited manuscripts at a publishing house of literary agency, which may feast indefinitely awaiting review. Some publishers do not have slush piles they return unsolicited work to author without review.

software   Programs that run on a computer. Word-processing software includes programs that enable writers to compose, edit, store, and print material.

special sales Sales of a book to appropriate retailers other than bookstores.

spine   That portion of the book's casing (or binding) that backs the bound page signatures and is visible when the volume is aligned on a bookshelf among other volumes.

stamping   In book publishing, the stamp is the impression of ornamental type and images (logo or monogram) on the books binding.

subsidiary rights   The reprint, serial, movie, and television, and audiotape and videotape rights deriving from a book. The division of profits between publisher and author from the sales of these rights is determined through negotiation.

subsidy publishing A mode of publication wherein the author pays a publishing company to produce his or her work, which may thus appear superficially to have been published conventionally.

suspense fiction   Fiction within a number of genre categories that emphasize suspense as well as usual literary techniques to keep the reader engaged.

syndicated column   Material publisher simultaneously in a number of newspapers or magazines.

synopsis   A summary in paragraph form, rather than in outline format. It is an important part of a book proposal.

T

table of contents A listing of a book's chapters and other sections; or of a magazine's articles and columns in the order in which they appear.

tabloid A smaller-than-standard-size newspaper (daily, weekly, monthly)

teleplay A screenplay geared toward television production.

terms The financial conditions agreed to in a book contract.

theme A general term for the underlying concept of a book.

thriller A novel of suspense with a plot structure that reinforces the elements of gamesmanship and the chase, with a sense of the hunt being paramount.

tip sheet An information sheet on a single book that presents general publication information, a brief synopsis of the book, information on relevant other books, and other pertinent marketing data such as author profile and advance blurbs.

title page The page at the front of a book that lists the title, subtitle, author, as well as the publishing house and sometimes its logo.

trade books Books distributed through the book trade- meaning bookstores and major book clubs.

trade discount The discount from the cover or list price that a publisher gives the bookseller. It is typically around 40%-50%.

trade list A catalog of all of a publisher's book in print, with ISBNs and order information.

trade (quality) paperbacks Reprints or original titles published in paperback format, larger in dimension than mass-market paperbacks, and distributed through regular retail book channels.

trade publishers Publishers of books for general readership. They are nonprofessional, nonacademic books that are distributed primarily through bookstores.

translation rights Rights sold either to a foreign agent or directly to a foreign publisher, either by author's agent or the original publisher.

treatment In screenwriting, a full narrative description of the story, including sample dialogue.

U

unauthorized biography A history of a person's life written without the consent or collaboration of the subject or the subjects survivors.

university press A publishing house affiliated with a sponsoring university. The university press is generally nonprofit and subsidized by the respective university.

unsolicited manuscript A manuscript sent to an editor or agent without being requested by the editor/agent.

V

vanity press A publisher that publishes books only at author's expense. They will generally agree to publish anything that is submitted and paid for.

W

word count The number of words in a given document; usually rounded off to the nearest 100.

Offical Contact Pages: Glossary

work-for-hire Writing done for an employer, or writing commissioned by a publisher or book packager who retains ownership of, and all rights pertaining to the written material.

Y

young-adult (YA) books Books for reader generally between the ages of 12 and 17.

young readers or younger readers Publishing terminology for the range of publications that address the earliest readers. Sometimes these books must hook the parents or caretakers who buy them.

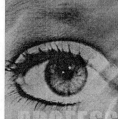

MARION
D E S I G N S
DESIGNS THAT SELL YOUR BUSINESS

PROFESSIONAL
AFFORDABLE
& WE DELIVER

WWW.MARIONDESIGNS.COM

COMPLETE CREATIVE DESIGN SERVICE: *Graphic Design & Professional Photography*

- Book Covers
- Bookmarks
- Business Cards
- Brochures
- Corporate ID
- CD Covers
- Logo Design
- Illustration
- Posters
- Printing
- Photography
- Web Design
- Etc.

Email: info@mariondesigns.com
Phone: 678.641.8689